Herwig Salmutter

Madmen led the Blind

Memoirs of an SS Obersturmführer

Herwig Salmutter

Madmen led the Blind

Memoirs of an SS Obersturmführer

Author

Herwig Salmutter, eldest son of Josef 'Sepp' Salmutter,
born 1943, British citizen,
residing with his wife Christine in London, UK
[for further details see chapter 'About the Author'.]

US Intelligence documents

The many quotes in this book are extracts
from US Intelligence documents and are grouped into

Inter-office documents
Eavesdropped conversation of POWs
Salmutter's handwritten Curriculum Vitae
Salmutter's written answers to a questionnaire

All eighty US Intelligence documents concerning
the POW Sepp Salmutter can be found at
https://hhsalmutter.wixsite.com/sepp1921

As my father likely would have wished,
the net profit from the sale of this book will go
to the medical humanitarian organization
Doctors Without Borders.

DEDICATION

Thanks to the skill and bravery of the Allied Forces defeating the Nazi dictatorship I was lucky to have had the opportunity to grow up in a free Austria.

Their victory and the subsequent establishment of a democratic political system combined with the Marshall Plan's immense economic aid allowed my generation of youngsters born during or just after the war to live in peace and prosperity.

My father, unfortunately, as will be shown in this story, did not have the same advantages and democratic freedoms in his youth as I had.

Herwig Salmutter

ENDORSEMENTS

EVERYTHING is extremely interesting to me. There is no comparable informative description of any of the 'Junker' [students] of the SS Medical Academy like his [Sepp Salmutter's] life and thus of these years.
Your very interesting manuscript indicates that your father wrote you lengthy letters. This gives the text great liveliness.
University Professor Dr.phil. Alois Kernbauer,
Karl-Franzens University Graz, Austria, Department of History;
published 'Die SS Ärztliche Akademie in Graz,1939-1945'
(‚The SS Medical Academy' in Graz 1939-1945)

CONTENTS

What do we know of our relatives
who fought for an unjust,
even criminal cause?

The search for relatives
is always a search for ourselves,
an exploration of boundaries,
identities and ambivalences.

In addition to curiosity,
it also takes courage
to deal with the past,
especially since it can be painful:
the beloved father...

Felix Römer, "Comrades"

THIS BOOK ALMOST WASN'T WRITTEN

It all started with the Corona virus lockdown, when I sorted out the attic and found a pile of half-forgotten papers my father had left me half a century ago; eighty US Intelligence documents that prvided evidence of my father's interrogations in 1945 at a US prison camp. How my father got his hands on these in 1969 remains a mystery, as they were still classified as a state secret. The Americans only opened their archives to historians in 2012; a few years later, a close family member of the Prisoner-of-War could request copies. In 2016, I obtained a set – identical to those my father had obtained more than 40 years earlier!

Back in 1969, a 26-year-old working in Africa, I didn't peruse my father's autobiographical notes. Mentally, I wasn't mature enough, and I was somewhat reluctant to deal with a former SS Obersturmführer's life before, during, and after the Nazi dictatorship.

Back then, I neither appreciated nor understood much of what my father had written about – SS medical and military academies, university life during the war, and the denazification process afterwards.

Later, going through the papers in the lockdown, I felt differently. I searched the internet, contacted the diocese in Graz-Seckau, the Styrian state archive, Graz University, and I met with one of the doctors who had worked with my father in Da Nang. I began to edit my father's autobiography, changing as little as possible to keep it aligned with his writing. With direct quotes from the interrogation notes, my father's story presents

> a unique record of an ordinary man
> living through extraordinary times.

All is in flux, nothing stays still. Shifting sand dune being part of the Eastern Erg in Algeria, 1969

FOREWORD

```
DAD DROWNED IN VIETNAM STOP
          FUNERAL ON JANUARY 17 STOP
                    PLEASE COME STOP MUM
```

In January 1970, I was living in Hassi Messaoud in the Algerian Sahara carrying out geophysical measurements on oil drilling rigs, when the above telegram from my mother arrived.

On the subsequent flight to Austria, my father's death was all I thought about. Could I have tried to get to know him better? Should I have spent more time with him and talked to him about his life? These and many more questions ran through my mind, without answers.

I reached Graz on Saturday, three days before the funeral. My father's coffin had arrived in Graz on Friday morning from South Vietnam, via San Francisco and Frankfurt/Main. Like thousands of their fallen, the Americans had embalmed my father in Vietnam. When the funeral home opened the coffin, my father lay there peacefully, looking as though he was merely asleep.

On Friday evening, there was a short news item about him on the TV station FS1. 'Graz doctor Josef Salmutter drowned in a swimming accident while serving on the Red Cross ship Helgoland.' The news accompanied a picture of my father's coffin placed between two uniformed Red Cross men.

3

My mother arranged a mass at the Old Catholic Church, although my father had left the church when he was eighteen. She insisted, 'the locals will be expecting it.' However, the local attendees were few in number, which was hardly surprising, given that my father had left Styria more than fifteen years earlier.

A representative of the German Red Cross told my mother that my father had suffered a heart attack while swimming in the sea. My father had waved his arms to attract the attention of his colleagues, but they couldn't save him. The Red Cross man gave us a metal chest containing my father's belongings - no personal clothing but books, a camera, developed films, and gifts for individual family members. My father had been packing in preparation for his holiday back home; one of the wrapped packages was addressed to me.
Yet, in that strange, slow chaos of funeral formalities, I had no time to open it and put it away in my suitcase.

I opened it after returning to Hassi Messaoud and discovered pages and pages in my father's handwriting, along with personal documents pressed between two hand painted wooden book covers.

Had the Americans been given access to my father's writings, they would undoubtedly have confiscated or destroyed all US Intelligence documents in his possession. Fortunately, it was the Red Cross, on the hospital ship in Vietnam where my father was working until his death, who had packed the chest containing his belongings. They transported it via Germany to Austria and handed it over to my mother. Thus, by a twist of fate, I received my father's message.

Atop the bundle was a folded piece of paper in a broader American format. It was an undated letter written to my father. The faded text was still readable:

Dear Sepp,

We followed your life since you were a prisoner-of-war at Fort Hunt and Wisconsin. To express our appreciation for you over the past 20 years, we decided to give you the papers documenting your interrogation in Fort Hunt 25 years ago. These include your answers to the 'Moral Questionnaire,' your interrogation transcripts, logs on eavesdropping, and the internal correspondence about your internment. All documents are stamped SECRET, but they now hold no further security value. At present, our staff in the US National Archives in College Park, Maryland, is copying hundreds of thousands of pages of documents like yours. You were one of 4,000 German prisoners of war who we observed in the camp. I believe there was mutual respect between you and your interrogator Captain Brown, who has since returned to his civilian profession as a lawyer. A visiting professor at university, he now lectures on dictatorships and the banality of evil. He is one of many who wish to publish the interrogation documents, and he can't wait to write a research paper on them. Mr. Brown has opponents who do not want to see his scholarly work published and prefer this knowledge remains limited to a few in the Intelligence community because 'the democratic prestige of the US takes precedence.' 'The US follows the laws of the Geneva Convention,' those Secret Service men maintain, 'and American Intelligence does not illegally eavesdrop on prisoners of war.'

Nevertheless, the pressure to publish is enormous and increasing with time. More than 20 years passed since these interrogations. We became trusted partners of the new democratic Germany, and the information collected from the prisoners remains only of personal or historical value. We are confident the records will soon be made available to historians.

Please, Sepp, don't forget, the enclosed documents are still classified. Keep them under strict lock and key, and don't expose them to strangers. None of them must yet fall into the hands of the public. We still have to remain anonymous; I can only hand over what you wrote at the time, what you said when the Secret Service bugged you, and some internal reports about you.

The psychological evaluations conducted at Fort Hunt found that you have no close friends, no drinking buddies, and are on your own. You write that, unlike your comrades, you didn't like going to the officers' mess. You are a loner. You became an orphan at three, and you have no siblings which influenced your development. To top that, you lived in a Catholic seminary suffering under crude educational methods. No wonder you remained introverted.

Be careful,
A friend

I folded the friend's note and set it aside. Leafing through the documents, photos, and papers, some of which were in my father's handwriting, I found a long letter addressed to me. I hesitated to read it for many reasons.

What had he wanted to tell me? Had he felt that we'd never had a serious conversation? Did he want to justify his behaviour to the family? Would he try to explain these documents or perhaps call them forgeries? Who was this 'friend' with access to these files in the US National Archives? An American or a mole? Had my father been blackmailed into keeping the truth about unpleasant past events out of the public domain? Did these documents – or anything in his past – have a link to his recent, sudden death?

Was this my father's autobiography? With some trepidation, I began to read...

PRISONER-OF-WAR CAMP, NAMUR

Dear Herwig,

Surprise, surprise, I am writing to you from South Vietnam, where I have been acclimatizing to the heat and humidity for the last four months. The vacancy of a trauma surgeon on the German Red Cross hospital ship Helgoland in Da Nang arrived at an ideal time for me, so I jumped at the chance. More about Vietnam later... right now, I want to explain what happened, totally out of the blue, how my past caught up with me, and what drove me to start writing my life story.

Every week, the Red Cross mailbag arrives from Germany on the ship. We sit in the canteen, and one of us – usually a cheerful but noisy little Bavarian nurse – yells out our names and distributes the mail. I had been here for three weeks and expected a modest handwritten envelope from your mother, as I had received the week before. Instead, she handed me a large, official brown package without a sender's name or address... from the United States! I knew it was something I didn't want my co-workers to see or inquire about, so I quietly brought it to my cabin. Inside I found classified reports from US Intelligence, documents relating to my past and my time in American captivity at the conclusion of WWII. They were badly Xeroxed copies, eighty in total. With apprehension, I started reading the oldest. It was from my time in Namur, Belgium, at my first prison camp...

...During the Battle of the Bulge on January 21, 1945, I ran over to the Americans. What compelled me to desert? Well, there were several reasons. My instinct for self-preservation told me that surviving in captivity was preferable to dying at the front. Furthermore, my lady friend Resi, whom I had last seen in November 1944, had advised me to do so. The Americans imprisoned me in their Namur camp from January 21 to April 5, 1945, where the Ritchie Boys* interrogated me during the first few weeks as a prisoner-of-war.

*The Ritchie Boys were a special US German-Austrian unit of Military Intelligence Service officers and enlisted men of World War II. They were trained at Camp Ritchie in Maryland. Many were German-speaking immigrants to the United States, often Jews who had fled Nazi persecution. Due to their German language and cultural knowledge, they primarily interrogated prisoners on the front lines and undertook counterintelligence work in Europe.

After my initial harsh interrogations, I began working for the American Intelligence FID in more welcoming surroundings.

> *'The POW is a young and intelligent Austrian doctor who deserted to the American forces. He is extremely cooperative and friendly. He has a magnetic personality. Seems to be very reliable. He worked for the FID in Namur from the end of January until April 5, 1945.' [office correspondence]*

Six weeks after my incarceration, I ran into our troop physician, Dr. Fronius, who was a prisoner like me and reminded me of something I already knew: If the Germans had caught me when I deserted...

> *'...the SS military court would have proceeded in the usual manner, i.e., sentencing to death and expulsion from the SS with shame and disgrace.' [Curriculum vitae]*

I spilled everything to the Yanks about my experiences and knowledge from the previous six years as a member of the Waffen SS. My great memory for detail enabled me *deserted and condemned to death by SS Kriegsgericht*

SECRET

Selected for: Z I

Date: 1 APRiL 45

Name: SALMUTTER, SEPP   3IG 2509053

Rank: 44 O/STURMFÜHRER

Unit: I/44 PZ ARTY.REGT 'DAS REICH'

Reason for selection: *S is a knowledgable med. officer - intelligent. Cooperative - can be used for many purposes - Furnished extensive report on KZ "Oranienburg", Government offices, Austria, answered Medical Questions, New weapons & SS straf-coy's. "Very reliable"*

HQ MFIU NO 1

Air
deserted and condemned to death by SS Kriegsgericht

SECRET

Selection for ZI   Date: 1 April 1945

Name: SALMUTTER, SEPP   3IG 2509053
Rank: SS O/STURMFÜHRER
Unit: I/SS PZ ARTY.REGT. 'DAS REICH'
Reason for selection: S is a knowledgable med. officer
-intelligent. Cooperative - can be used for many puposes-
Furnished extensive report on KZ "Oranienburg",
Government Offices, Austria, answered Medical Ques-
tions, New weapons, SS-Straf-comp's, "Very reliable".
            HQ MFIU NO1
        FID MTS
            APO 887   US ARMY
                    Leo Attlee, 1st Lt. OS

**In Belgium, Salmutter became POW - US Prisoner-of-war.
First Lieutenant Leo Attlee had been pleased
with his knowledge and cooperation with
US intelligence and arranged his transfer to America.**

to report on specific people I had encountered during my military career, including students at the University of Graz, participants at the SS Military Academies, commanders of three concentration camps, and army superiors.

I inundated the Yanks with information, and they greedily took it all in. I was only a twenty-three-year-old and they pardoned me. In the end, I was a good catch for US Intelligence and brought laurels to the interrogation officer. First Lieutenant Leo Attlee was so impressed that he arranged my transfer to the United States. I liked him and felt sure he would go on to have a successful military career.

Lieutenant Walter 'Just call me Walt' Kerr interrogated me for weeks. Every morning, he said to me, *'Good 'n tight, like a German virgin.'* To him, it must have sounded like *'Guten Tag.'* We conversed in slow English, and he took copious notes. It took some time for me to pick up his Texan slang. We could have become pals under different circumstances. He was around 40 years old, had short brown hair, wore reading glasses, and wasn't overly ambitious. He'd got cases of Merlot from who knows where and kept them stashed in his office, where we drank together from metal cups. 'When it's all over, you'll come to Lubbock,' he said. 'You will be our guest of honor and my family and friends will welcome you to a barbecue, where you can eat huge Texas steaks hanging over the edge of your plate.' Thinking about it now, I tell myself I should visit Walt one of these days.

Now, Herwig, my thoughts go back to my time in Fort Hunt, Virginia, USA. There they forced me to reflect on my entire life – not just to recount it to the Americans but also to scrutinize the past in my mind. What had I been thinking and feeling at the time?

US INTERROGATION CENTER, FORT HUNT

April 9, 1945 was the date of my first flight. What a fantastic adventure! We had to board a DC3, the Air Force mule in Paris. When the plane is on the runway, the floor is on a slant; the seats all level out once the plane is in the air. France soon faded from view, and the Atlantic waves flickered below us, where German and enemy submarines continued to sink each other. Because of the six-hour time difference, we arrived at the military airport in Washington in the evening, having left Paris around lunchtime. We boarded a coach with blacked-out windows without knowing where we were going or what would happen to us.

As we exited the coach, a line of American soldiers in khaki uniforms met us. They kept submachine guns leveled at us and held guard dogs on leashes. Our squad was composed of troops from several European fronts; they ranged from 18 to 45, mostly young. Some had fought throughout the war, while others, like me, had only been in action since late 1944, aside from my uneventful campaign in France in 1940.

Americans classified us as Nazi supporters or anti-Nazis. They directed me to the anti-Nazi group for reasons I don't understand; I certainly didn't know the criteria by which the Americans chose us to be flown out here. Was it because we were skilled engineers and researchers? Was I there because I was educated and cooperative? Or because I had contacts in the concentration camps? Had I worked so amicably with US Intelligence in Namur that Walt had sent my name up the chain to his boss, Leo, and gotten me an American ticket as a 'thank you'? How could someone be a member of the SS and an anti-Nazi?

Looking around, I noticed my new surroundings were similar to those where I had spent the previous two and a half months in Namur: twin barbed-wire fences and gates, high watchtowers with armed guards, and wooden barracks. Our field of vision was obstructed by a forest. A substantial brick structure stood in the center of the camp. From a watchtower, a soldier holding a machine gun stared down on the camp, scrutinizing us. I later discovered this building was a cross-shaped complex, like a swastika without the hooks; only Germans would have made such an association. American Intelligence agents with headphones and tape recorders sat in another hut, which I couldn't see from where I was standing. Later, I learned that, in violation of the Geneva Convention, they were listening in on German inmates in their cells and recording their conversations as they discussed their war experiences and personal problems.

We were brought single-file down the stone building's long corridor and ordered to sit on an uncomfortable wooden bench. The guards summoned us alphabetically and led us to an adjoining room, where we identified ourselves to an officer and turned over any papers we still had on us. After he took some notes and gathered the documents, a guard led us to a changing room, where an army doctor inspected us. Next, a flunky handed us prisoner outfits. Three white letters glistened on the chest of my shirt and the blue trouser legs: POW – prisoner-of-war. An armed guard brought me to my cell. It was a medium-sized room with a high ceiling, two beds, two seats, and a wall-mounted table. The sun would shine in during the day through a barred south-facing window. My cellmate came not long after I got settled: Erwin Thomas from Vienna was the next name in the alphabet. We would stay together and be interrogated for the next three weeks before being removed to another POW camp elsewhere in the United States.

The US Army Command identified Fort Hunt by a mailbox number, 'PO Box 1142 '. The Geneva Convention requires all prisoner camps to provide the names of detainees to the Red Cross but the Americans worked around this requirement by designating Fort Hunt as a Temporary Detention Center, which kept it out of the category of officially registered POW camps. No prisoner at Fort Hunt was allowed to contact his family back home. The Americans did not register us, and we were labeled as MIA until they'd interrogated and transported us to other camps. Only later did they inform our families of our status.

This concealment was necessary for the Americans. If they had learned of German war crimes while eavesdropping on prisoners' conversations, they would have been unable to prosecute, as they were committing a war crime of a different kind. Reports of the executions of American POWs who had fallen into the hands of the Germans went unpunished; the courts in the United States, Germany, or any other country where these soldiers had fought during the war did not prosecute these and other war crimes perpetrated by the Germans. All papers, including mine, are now housed in the United States National Archives in College Park, Maryland, labeled 'classified.' Troops who actively participated in murders and massacres returned

Photo: mug shot, US Intelligence, 1945

SECRET

Report of Interrogation :

P/W   : SALMUTTER, Sepp
Rank   : 1st Lt. SS
Unit   : 1 Obt.Pz.Arty.Regt.Das Reich
Captd : Geary/Belgium, 21 January 1945.

Veracity : Believed reliable.

SECRET

BASIC PERSONNEL RECORD
(Alien Enemy or Prisoner of War)

31G-2509053

SALMUTTER, Sepp
(Name of Internee)

Male
(Sex)

F. P. C. :

Height 5 ft. 7 in.

Weight 140

Eyes   Brown

Skin   Fair

Hair   Brown

Age   24

Distinguishing marks or characteristics:

4. On scar on right thigh.

Reference :

INVENTORY OF PERSONAL EFFECTS TAKEN FROM INTERNEE

1.
2.
3.
4.
5.
6.
7.
8.
9.

The
(Signature of internee)

(Date and place where internee is to be released (Army enclosure, naval station, or other place))

RIGHT HAND

1. Thumb	2. Index finger	3. Middle finger	4. Ring finger	5. Little finger

LEFT HAND

6. Thumb	7. Index finger	8. Middle finger	9. Ring finger	10. Little finger

W. D., P. M. G. Form No. 2

SECRET

US Intelligence personnel file on Sepp Salmutter, 1945

home with no marks against their character to resume their careers as teachers, judges, and so on. You might be wondering, Herwig, why the Americans worked so hard to gain information on which they couldn't act. I'll go into more detail about it later in my story.

For many years, the American officers, secretaries, and other support workers at Fort Hunt swore strict secrecy. None of their relatives had any idea what they did. American officials never acknowledged the existence of Fort Hunt and the interrogation of German captives. I am not aware of any historical or biographical research mentioning this camp.

Erwin never suspected the Americans of bugging our cell, whereas I was wary from the start. Arriving aboard a bus with blacked-out windows was the first thing arousing my suspicion. I thought there was more to it, and it turned out I was correct.

Therefore, I chatted to my cellmate as generally as possible, engaging in benign conversation about my life. The Americans were not stupid, and if it appeared I had nothing to hide, they would have been suspicious. So, I purposefully incriminated myself during chats with Erwin, but only slightly. I told him the truth that I had met Reichsführer SS Heinrich Himmler at the SS Military Academy's graduation party in Tölz.

> *'I have spoken to Himmler… he is very nice when you talk to him man to man.' [eavesdropped]*

I also told Erwin that I didn't believe in the Nazis' racial ideology. To demonstrate this, I explained that I had married someone with a questionable Aryan background, against the wishes of the SS. It wasn't true, but I wanted the Americans listening in to believe it, so that I would be viewed well by them. I didn't care if I lied or not; I just wanted to get through my imprisonment as safely as possible. Another time I told Erwin:

'I would forbid my daughters to marry a Negro, but that is no reason to destroy the whole race.' [eavesdropped]

All convicts at Fort Hunt were required to complete the 'Moral Questionnaire', which consisted of printed questions. Extra pages were available, if necessary, to further clarify their responses. It asked questions like: How do you feel about Hitler? When and how do you believe the war will end? What lands would the new German borders contain? How can the Germans be re-educated, that is, educated to support democracy? What should the punishment be for war criminals? Did you know any opponents of the Nazis? What are your thoughts on the various political parties that would be allowed in the new Germany and Austria, on the church's position, and the Jewish question?

According to international law, we only had to provide the bare minimum of information; we should not have been interrogated as prisoners. It was no concern to me; I preferred to be eavesdropped on and questioned by Americans rather than slaughtered mercilessly or put on trial in Russian captivity.

In our cell, Erwin and I spoke about everything under the sun. I taught him English, and we read the camp newspaper, printed in German which included the most recent news, carefully edited from an American perspective.

A guard would unlock the door several times a day and take one of us away for more questioning by a US officer, often the same person day after day. It was not permitted to begin the interrogation with the 'Heil Hitler' salute, which had become a habit for most of us, if not all. For some, it was more than that; incomprehensibly, a small minority of us, undeterred by the fact we were now US prisoners, remained steadfastly faithful to Nazi habits.

What would the Americans think of me? What did they expect of me? I had no idea. Whatever it was, I was willing to cooperate. I was going to help them, but I also had to be careful not to make things worse for myself in the process.

My interrogator, Captain Brown, spoke good German and questioned me point by point on my written responses to the Moral Questionnaire. Despite his authority, he was kind and courteous and exuded a sense of tranquility. Behind him on the wall was a framed photograph of Roosevelt, though Harry Truman had been elected President of the United States a few days before our arrival at Fort Hunt. My interrogator sat in a luxurious swivel chair behind a metal US Army desk while I sat on a plain seat across from the desk. He chain-smoked throughout the interrogations and offered me Lucky Strikes to maintain a positive atmosphere.

He exhibited disbelief at some of my comments, or claimed not to comprehend the links. He probed and tried to trap me in contradictions on multiple occasions.

> *'Some things in my curriculum vitae were unclear, he said. He didn't believe the reasons I had given for joining the SS. He asked me where I was in May 1941. He wanted to check if I had written everything down truthfully.'* [eavesdropped]

I discovered that he knew a lot more about the SS Panzer Division 'Das Reich' than I did.

> *'They knew everything – every little detail about my Division.'* [eavesdropped]

I liked the Yanks back then, and I still like them now, despite having been adversaries. Although we occasionally had heated debates, Captain Brown respectfully interrogated me. I told him multiple times that it would be impossible for him to put himself in my shoes, since no one truly knows whether they will act like a hero, or otherwise, when the moment comes. I believe he grew to look forward to our meetings. Despite his chilly indifference during the interrogations, he had a favorable view of me, according to internal office communication only available to me now:

> *'The POW is an alert, intelligent young Austrian who joined the SS to attend the SS Medical Academy in his hometown of GRAZ to continue his studies. He is vehemently anti-Nazi and is reliable. His typical Austrian behavior, his marriage to a non-Aryan, and finally his desertion to the Americans secured him a dishonorable discharge and a death sentence [by the SS].'* [office correspondence]

During the interrogations, the Americans were curious about our political views. They also took note of what we said when we thought the two of us were alone. The following is a sample from a conversation I had with Erwin, which the Americans taped and transcribed.

Gesetz zur Verhütung erbkranken Nachwuchses.
Vom 14. Juli 1933.

Die Reichsregierung hat das folgende Gesetz beschlossen, das hiermit verkündet wird:

§ 1

(1) Wer erbkrank ist, kann durch chirurgischen Eingriff unfruchtbar gemacht (sterilisiert) werden, wenn nach den Erfahrungen der ärztlichen Wissenschaft mit großer Wahrscheinlichkeit zu erwarten ist, daß seine Nachkommen an schweren körperlichen oder geistigen Erbschäden leiden werden.

(2) Erbkrank im Sinne dieses Gesetzes ist, wer an einer der folgenden Krankheiten leidet:

1. angeborenem Schwachsinn,
2. Schizophrenie,
3. zirkulärem (manisch-depressivem) Irresein,
4. erblicher Fallsucht,
5. erblichem Veitstanz (Huntingtonsche Chorea),
6. erblicher Blindheit,
7. erblicher Taubheit,
8. schwerer erblicher körperlicher Mißbildung.

(3) Ferner kann unfruchtbar gemacht werden, wer an schwerem Alkoholismus leidet.

The 1933 law created a large number of "Genetic Health Courts", consisting of a judge, a medical officer, and medical practitioner, which "shall decide at its own discretion after considering the results of the whole proceedings and the evidence tendered".

There were three amendments by 1935. The most significant changes allowed the Higher Court to renounce a patient's right to appeal, and to fine physicians who did not report patients who they knew would qualify for sterilisation under the law.

Law for the Prevention of Genetically Diseased Offspring, issued 14th July 1933

The Reich Government has passed the following Law, which is hereby promulgated:

§1

(1) Any person suffering from a hereditary disease may be rendered incapable of procreation by means of a surgical operation (sterilization), if the experience of medical science shows that it is highly probable that his descendants would suffer from some serious physical or mental hereditary defect.

(2) For the purposes of this law, any person will be considered as hereditarily diseased who is suffering from any one of the following diseases:

1. Congenital Mental Deficiency,
2. Schizophrenia,
3 . Manic-Depressive Insanity,
4. Hereditary Epilepsy,
5. Hereditary Chorea (Huntington's),
6. Hereditary Blindness,
7. Hereditary Deafness,
8. Any severe hereditary deformity.

(3) Any person suffering from severe alcoholism may be also rendered incapable of procreation.

*Sepp Salmutter had been indoctrinated
at university with Nazi ideas on the subject
of the prevention of genetically deceased offspring.
Sadly, he blindly followed and supported the then
enforced law of the land
which had been led by madmen.*

Imagine how I felt decades later, reading my words taken illicitly down and archived!

> *'When one thinks about it now, one has to admit that one has gone a little bit against the humanity of the 20th century.'* [eavesdropped]

From the vantage point of today, Herwig, I made a terrible and heinous comment. In 1945, I still knew nothing of the Nazi atrocities, whether at the front by the Waffen SS, in concentration camps by doctors, or the numerous other crimes done by the Nazis.

We all had been unquestionably faithful to the Nazi dictatorship; we had pledged allegiance to Adolf Hitler and couldn't simply act against such an oath overnight. In the end, we only knew the National Socialists' point of view. The whole point of being brainwashed is that you don't notice it happening. You have no idea which pieces of your soul are no longer yours but theirs.

This thought brings me to one of the worst parts of my biography and the darkest chapter in Germany's history, explicitly concerning German doctors. At Fort Hunt, when I answered questions regarding the German health service, I had already defected from the Waffen SS and left the Nazi regime behind me. Their ideas to eradicate inherited congenital disabilities through sterilization, known as eugenics, had been taught at Graz University as part of my medical education, and then reinforced by what I had learned at the SS Military Academies. To my shame, they continued to influence me for several years after the war.

The National Socialists twisted Friedrich Nietzsche's concept of Superman (Übermensch) into the concept of a physiologically superior Aryan master race. After taking power in 1933, Hitler enacted the 'Law for the Prevention of Genetically Diseased Offspring.' The Nazis subsequently selected who was 'worthy of life.' The rule required sterilizing people with congenital mental defects, schizophrenia, manic - depressive psychosis, hereditary epilepsy, and severe drunkenness. It included the deaf, the blind, and others with congenital physical disabilities. Aside from sterilization, Nazi doctors killed over one hundred thousand Germans deemed 'unworthy of life' in medical institutions and, in some instances, isolated mansions and castles. The authorities imprisoned and murdered inmates against the wishes of their closest kin.

Although I supported the sterilization of diseased offspring at the time, I had no concept of the inhumane extremes to which some Nazi medics had sunk, and I now fully condemn these notions. My statement, which I made in US captivity nearly 25 years ago, now disgusts and mortifies me. It shows the depths to which I had fallen when I described and extolled the efficiency of the German health service, as follows:

> 'The overall health management of the German people has been raised to a significant level, but mainly due to increased interest in the military fitness of the people. That is to say:
> * Fitness for marriage: examination before marriage with a possible refusal of marriage in justified cases.
> * Eradication of the possibility of diseased offspring by sterilizing people with severe physical or mental genetic defects.

Extensive and intensive infant care and maternal counseling at state expense, resulting in a sharp drop in infant mortality and rates of rickets.
Ensuring time and space for health-promoting sporting activities for all working classes, especially the youth.'
[questionnaire]

Nevertheless, I was also opposed to the Nazi regime:

'German nature is not National Socialism. Concentration camps are un-German. For me, Goethe and Schiller represent Germany – the real German spirit.' [eavesdropped]

Most inmates shared my view on the National Socialist system, believing it to have positive and negative aspects.

Let me now move on to less contentious occurrences in my life. I hope you find these sections interesting, as I would like to tell you about our relatives and my childhood.

MY BIRTH

I had to tell the Americans my life story, so I began with my birth, carefully considering what I could mention, what I should include, and what I should leave out. For you, however, I'll paint the entire picture truthfully.

I was born on January 31, 1921, at noon. My birthplace was Semriach 44, in the province of Styria, near Graz, where my mother and widowed grandmother lived. The next day at two o'clock in the afternoon, the church christened me as a Roman Catholic.

Preparing my CV for the Americans I wrote:

> 'When I was three years old, my mother died. My grandmother, Amalia Salmutter, took over my upbringing in Niederschöckl, near Graz, after my father had remarried.' [Curriculum vitae]

The truth was more complicated: I was born out of wedlock. My baptismal certificate bears only my mother's name. I kept that back from the US interrogators. Being an illegitimate child weighed heavily on me. People didn't talk about being born to an unmarried mother; they would have labeled me a bastard if they had. Therefore, I kept quiet about the subject.

My mother died of a stomach ulcer when she was twenty-eight years old, before she could have told me about my father. My grandmother may not have known who he was. Perhaps she wanted to protect me from unwelcome rumors. She was 53 years old, and I was three when she took over my upbringing. It was difficult for both of us.

I want to tell you more about my childhood before this period of my life was forgotten. If I don't describe it in detail now, it may be lost from our family history forever.

Despite having no brothers or sisters, I enjoyed a pleasant upbringing that inspired and molded my personality. As a child, I was shielded from the wider world. The conditions of my early years are hard to imagine nowadays, but I became determined to study, hoping to escape poverty.

Sepp Salmutter's birth certificate:
He had been born illegitimate
and the identity of his father remains unclear

OUR FAMILY FARM

Niederschöckl is about a two-hour walk from Graz. There are nine ancient farmhouses on either side of the village road, which winds like an 'S' from north-east to south-west. The local church and school are one kilometer away, perched on a hill between the communities of Niederschöckl and Oberschöckl. Standing next to the farm, I had an uninterrupted view of the 1445 m high Schöckl mountain, where winter made its presence known with the first snowfall. The village is located about 500 meters above sea level.

When needed, everyone in the village community aided and supported one another. Everyday life was more or less constant; no one moved in, and no one moved out. We Salmutters were the only newcomers. Perhaps it was my imagination, but I often felt different from the other kids; we led a life linked to the seasons, with plenty of freedom to play. We could run around the hamlet, play hide-and-seek in barns, climb over farm carts and our playmates' parents welcomed us inside their homes.

Farmers' families had generally two or three children. The first child took over their parent's farm, the second married a spouse with a farm, and the third had to leave to find employment elsewhere, in a factory or as a farmhand or maid on one of the neighboring farms, or else to make a living as a tailor, cobbler, merchant, carpenter, or builder.

Every day, the postman came. Despite rarely having mail to distribute, he always brought the Graz-based Kleine Zeitung, our daily source of local and international news. A serialized book — a romance or a crime thriller — took up one-third of the penultimate page, and half of the inhabitants of Styria anxiously followed this part. I could often hear locals discussing the heroes' foolishness, deception, or passion in the stories as if they were actual acquaintances.

My next-door neighbor kept a vicious St. Bernard barking and baring its teeth anytime I came over. Fortunately, a chain restrained the beast short of the farmhouse gate; given its size, it might have knocked down an adult man. Before I could go past him, the farmer or his wife had to yell, 'Into the cabin, Nero!' People observed the year's passage not in months but via the celebrations of the Catholic Church. We didn't say 'early November' but 'after All Saints' Day'; we didn't say 'late August' but 'after the Assumption of Mary.' On January 6, the holy day of Epiphany, carol singers dressed as the Magi from the East arrived at the farmhouses, as had been the tradition for 500 years. Young monastic students walked from house to house in song, conveying the joyous Christmas message to the people in exchange for alms, which could be money or food. They drew the blessing C+M+B — Christus mansionem benedicat, or 'Christ bless this house' — on all the doors of dwellings and stables. This inscription, applied with white chalk, stayed up all year, in the expectation it would keep evil at bay.

Like all small children, I was terrified of Krampus, the devil in black who accompanied Saint Nicholas on December 6, with his big red tongue hanging down and his hands rattling a thick chain. He carried on his back a wicker basket and was ready to steal away naughty kids who had misbehaved throughout the previous year.

In June 1930, at the age of nine, I received my First Holy Communion at the pilgrim church of Maria-Trost in Graz. I recall standing in the middle of my class wearing a white shirt and shorts, holding a gold-decorated candle in my hand. Terror gripped me as I glanced up at the two towers following the swiftly moving clouds over the dark blue sky. I feared the entire church would tumble over me.

Many disjointed scenes come back to me when I think about my time in Niederschöckl. I recall jumping into the village pond where fat toads and small water snakes swam and capturing lizards, grass frogs, and grass snakes to scare other kids by slipping them down the backs of their shirts. I remember the cesspit next to our house all too well. Our game was to place a large flat plank over it and balance our way across. In one instance, I fell in, barely clinging to the board. Grandmother threw up her hands in horror at such folly. I stank like manure for days, even after being doused with countless buckets from the well.

We built dams across the creek beside our house when spring arrived, as you would do a generation later. We blocked the river with branches, large stones, and boards if we could find them, swam in the deepening pool, and fished for tadpoles and sticklebacks. I directed the excess water over a mill wheel I had fashioned from an empty wooden yarn spool from my uncle's cobbler's shop. It was a different era, and an orphaned peasant boy had few options

Salmutters' farm house in Niederschòckl, 1948
The family lived in poverty as in the 19th century

for entertainment. I know you didn't have it much better as a kid, Herwig, and you and your pals also wandered around barefoot in the spring, summer, and autumn. Do you recall jumping into the same village pond as a child? I'm not sure if there were any toads or snakes left.

My task throughout the summer was to carry homemade apple cider to the farmhand, Alois, and my uncle, who were working in the field. I would fill a jug from the wooden cask in the cellar and walk fifteen minutes to their site. When they had finished drinking from the pitcher, I protected it with a cloth thrown over to keep flies away and set it in the shade of a tree.

When winter arrived, and enough snow had covered the ground, the village children spent their free time sledding and skiing. We slid into old-fashioned leather bindings to keep our high boots on the long skis. The first thing we did was construct a little ski jump to compete with one another. Frequently we fell, but I don't recall anyone breaking a bone, although bruises were common. Before removing the thick winter boots, I would have to scrape the ice off my shoelaces back at home.

No doctor ever visited the village, though a veterinarian came. Some locals became well-versed in traditional medicine, collecting various herbs and roots to use – fresh, dried, or pickled. Years of hard labor had left older farmers with crooked backs, swollen legs, missing teeth, and the shakes. I assumed it was customary for many of them to languish undetected and isolated from the active community. In addition to the elderly, there were First World War invalids, some of whom had lost multiple limbs.

As I mentioned before, you and I shared a similar childhood, growing up in the same village and attending the same school. Frau Mejak was our teacher at the rural school. Both of us looked forward to getting educated. Because there were so few children, the building had only three rooms for eight classes. Frau Mejak taught the first and second terms in the same room simultaneously, which always went off smoothly. I'm sure you remember her with the same fondness as I do.

On our route to school, we had to cross the local brook. The creek swelled so much with snowmelt in the spring that the old wooden bridge would become inundated, and we'd return home with soaking wet feet and clothes. We could leave class early on the hottest days of summer, which we all enjoyed, playing football on a flat meadow! In winter, we wore shorts and thick woolen stockings held up by elastic suspenders and loosely inserted buttons. Long pants were reserved for skiing. I used to wonder how grown-ups could put up with wearing long pants all year. I didn't receive my first pair until after I left Niederschöckl.

Few people in the village exchanged money. Instead, we bartered with agricultural produce. A magician who performed at school was paid with eggs. Homemade sausages or hams counted as a favored form of payment.

My grandmother was a strong woman; her wedding, only six weeks before the birth of her first child, would suggest she was unsure if her future husband would be the correct choice. She bore him seven children, and he died shortly after the last delivery. She had married into the Salmutter family and, as a widow, after eight years of matrimony, was still regarded as an outsider. Though her husband, brother-in-law, and father-in-law practiced as tailors, neither of her two surviving children followed in their family's footsteps. My mother assisted my grandmother around the house and, on occasion, worked as a waitress at the local inn. Grandmother's son Friedrich became a licensed shoemaker. The extended Salmutter family begrudged my grandmother's inheritance, which probably explains why, after my mother's early death, she turned her back on all their nagging and envy and left Semriach. Her refusal to yield to the wishes of her in-laws and be manipulated by them shows her strength of will. Life was not easy for single women with children, and it could not have been an easy decision to sell her home and seek a better fortune.

With the proceeds from the sale of the Semriach estate in 1926, my grandmother acquired a modest farm in Niederschöckl, about ten miles away, in equal shares with her son Friedrich. They had cultivated a little land around their house, though this hardly qualified them as farmers. But, living in Semriach, surrounded by farms, one couldn't help but learn a lot about agriculture. Although Friedrich stuck to his profession as the village shoemaker, he worked part-time as a small farmer on the purchased land. As a cobbler, he mended the long leather belts that powered the threshing machines, or he would make shoes to measure, using discarded straps for soles. The machines ran all day at harvest time, and uncle Friedrich did the necessary repairs overnight.

My grandmother, uncle Friedrich, and the farmhand Alois managed the farm. The farmhouse was a dilapidated structure covered with red tiles. The first floor held a kitchen, two bedrooms, and the cobbler's shop; Alois lived above, beneath the roof. There was no such thing as a separate living room. Because the house stood on a slant, the cellar and stables could be accessed from the outside, though one had to avoid the cesspit and dung mound on the left. From the kitchen, through a descending stairway, I could enter the cellar where the farm animals slept at night and where swallows built their nests in the warmer months. As a child, I was terrified of ghosts whenever I walked on the slick stone staircase leading down to the cellar. When I needed to get cider from the barrel, I would dash down the steps and back up again, as fast as my legs could carry me – holding the paraffin lantern in one hand and the jug in the other.

The toilet was a small hut set away from the house, with a heart cut out in the lockable door. Ripped newspaper strips hung on the wall on a nail, and a wooden lid covered the hole. Alois regularly emptied the pit underneath, scattering the contents across the fields.

Adjacent to the toilet stood rabbit hutches on posts, with three pens below and three above, all set at a reasonable height for feeding the rabbits and cleaning out the cages. The chicken coop, a covered firewood rack, and a chopping block were nearby. In cooler seasons, when the weather was unsuitable for extensive fieldwork, Alois sawed, chopped, and split the logs he had fetched from the forest for the kitchen stove.

Several cats prowled around the kitchen, curling up on a chair, a wall ledge, or the table. They relished the warmth of my grandmother's wood-burning stove, which also served as a source of heat in the winter. Apart from milk, the cats got nothing; they needed to forage for a living by hunting mice. Going around the home inspecting the mouse traps, removing any dead mice, replenishing the lures with bacon, and reloading them was one of my regular chores. From an early age, farm boys learn how to deal with deceased animals, from trapped mice to slaughtered pigs.

Grandmother fed coarsely crushed maize to the chickens outside the front door. As soon as she hit the feed bowl with a metal spoon, the clucking chickens approached – half running, half flying – and immediately began pecking. She tricked the hens into going broody by putting plaster eggs beneath them, and then removing one plaster egg from the nest for each successive egg laid in the following days. Was this a lesson to be learned later in life: how to deceive for profit?

I fed the hens with maybugs, which I shook down in the early morning cold from the plum trees. The chickens would swallow the immobile bugs before they'd warmed themselves in the first rays of light. Every four years the village experienced a maybug plague.

We slept soundly on beds made from linen sacks stuffed every autumn with fresh maize leaves. The inside walls of the house were rough plastered, and over time smoke from the wood-fired stove discolored them. The kitchen walls and ceiling had to be painted every summer from top to bottom with white lime diluted with water. Uncle also used lime as mortar for building repairs. He dug a pit next to grandmother's garden, filled it with water, and poured bags of burnt lime into it. He surrounded the pit with boards to prevent people from falling in; whenever necessary, my uncle would take a ladle full of the soft mass from the hole, ready for use.

To make myself useful in the evenings, I lit the paraffin lamp in the kitchen. It had a side mirror and hung on a wall nail. First, I turned up the wick, lit it with matches, then slowly turned it back until the lamp flickered weakly. I put on the glass cylinder with its lower belly, and the lamp began to shine brightly. With the small wick drive wheel, I could regulate the brightness. Once a week, when the paraffin in the glass reservoir became too low for the wick, I would refill it from a tightly sealed canister. I learned early on that handling paraffin was dangerous when close to a fire. The fact I was allowed to light and refill the lamp was a source of secret pride; it showed the family could depend on me to carry out such critical domestic tasks.

A trader came to the village every Tuesday. He sold flour, sugar, bottled beer, mustard, socks, house wares, cleaning supplies, and other goods. We didn't have to go out and buy fruit, milk, butter, honey, or jam because we remained self-sufficient in providing these items, or we might acquire them from a neighbor. We made our own bread, and grandmother churned the cream from the top of the milk into butter in a tall, wooden barrel. She devoted herself to tending her vegetable garden from spring to autumn, where she cultivated various plants, so there was always something to harvest. These served as the foundation of our diet. She grew beetroot, lettuce, cabbage, cucumbers, radishes, gooseberries, red and black currants, strawberries, onions, garlic, carrots, beans, peas, mint, parsley, chives, and medicinal herbs such as sage, rosehip, chamomile, and St. John's Wort in her garden, which separated our house from the village street.

Fruit grew abundantly around the property. We picked cherries from a massive tree in front of the house, as well as apples, pears, apricots, plums, hazelnuts, and walnuts from surrounding trees and saved some of our harvested fruit for the winter months. In late spring, we concocted a brown, syrupy walnut brandy from not-quite-ripe walnuts in their thick green skins, soaked in clear alcohol with additional sugar, and let it stand for two months in a sunny window.

Meadow flowers bloomed in brilliant colors in the summer, and I enjoyed picking them to fill a tin vase and arranging them on my grandmother's dining table. The meadows were home to a plethora of gastronomic goodies. We harvested the young shoots and leaves of wild nettles, washed and flattened them with a rolling pin, and made creamed spinach. Before the yellow blossom developed, we plucked the upper rosette leaves of dandelions in the spring to eat as a salad green – a great treat. When I chewed the leaves of the sorrel plant, they generated a sour flavor I loved. I fondly recall the plucked elderflowers, dipped in batter and fried to a crisp in lard.

On Sunday mornings, when we returned home from church, I would see middle-aged men and ladies – dressed in knickerbockers, colorful socks, traditional jackets, hiking boots, and hats – carrying walking sticks and strolling past our house. 'City folk stretching their legs,' uncle explained. They descended the trail from the Maria-Trost pilgrims' chapel toward Niederschöckl, crossing a hill topped by a tavern. Ours was the last farmhouse on the ascending village road, where Tivoli Lane splits off, leading up to the Tivoli Inn, a further 15-minute walk through fields and forest. Some trekkers held maps, while others asked me for directions or requested water from our draw well. 'Delicious water, so refreshing,' they exclaimed, sometimes handing me a schilling, with which I would buy a small bar of chocolate from the weekly vendor. The day-hikers dined at the Tivoli Inn on farmers' bacon and cheese, locally baked bread, and schnitzels with green salad, accompanied by cider or beer and followed by pastry and coffee, all the while admiring the magnificent view of the hilly Styrian countryside, our village sitting proudly in the foreground.

We country kids ran around barefoot, clad in lederhosen and braces, filthy but healthy and cheerful. The hikers regarded us the same way we now look at children in the Third World today. For them, we represented impoverished Styrians who had to make do without electricity and with manual water pumps. The hikers struck me as the weird ones, squandering their time so frivolously! Who needed to stretch their legs with so much to be done? Our two worlds collided here – my quiet, familiar village and the bustling city of the hill walkers.

Herwig, I don't want to leave you with this description of my childhood. My memories of our time on the farm in Niederschöckl would be incomplete without Alois, the farmhand.

MY CHILDHOOD WITH ALOIS

My fifty-five-year-old grandmother bought the Nieder-schöckl property with Alois as a sitting tenant. Alois had worked for the previous owner and knew the farm, the stable animals, the agricultural equipment, and the surrounding fields, making him an invaluable asset.

When I moved to Niederschöckl with my grandmother and uncle Friedrich, I was five years old, and Alois was about twenty-five. He wore short blond hair and was of a muscular build; he came from Kumberg, which was an hour's walk away, was unmarried, pleasant, and hardy – oh, and he was big. Uncle stitched custom-made shoes for his oversized feet.

As a child, my grandmother forbade me from drinking cider, even though I didn't enjoy the taste. Parents in Styria gave wailing babies diluted cider to keep them quiet. Alcohol damaged many children's brains, and it seemed likely Alois' brain had been harmed. True, he wasn't the sharpest tool in the drawer, but he was a tireless worker and advisor, who showed no intention or desire to play the boss. Alois understood crop cycles, the annual rotation of potatoes, maize, rye, and wheat, which land to keep for meadows, how to deal with freshwater springs forming damp patches and creeks in the grasslands, and where to grow apple, pear, plum and cherry trees. He knew when and how to apply liquid manure and dung to the grasslands and fields.

Thinking about it, I realize I spent most of my time with Alois. I used to run all day behind him in my preschool years.

Water pump with hand swivel
The whole village lived without running water

Alois was the same age as my village friends' fathers and enjoyed teaching me new things and afterward quizzing me. When I was five years old, I was too small to harness the ox and couldn't lift the collar over the ox's head, yet he still gave me the reins to steer the oxcart.

Alois kept the farm running and repaired the wagon wheels when needed. He did this by removing the outer iron ring, replacing the damaged spokes, smearing grease on the wheel axles, and remounting the assembled wheel back onto the wagon. I could help, it felt good to squeeze the stiff grease through my fingers, like damp clay after rain between my bare toes. Alois also repaired the barn door, replaced broken roof tiles, fixed the chimney and lightning conductor, and mended the tall ladders used for cherry-picking. In addition, he cut my hair.

Because there was no electric power, the farmers threshed the grain in the barn with wooden flails, creating a lot of noise and dust, and as far as I recall, it was at the hottest time of year. Young men from a neighboring village, recruited by my grandmother, sweated and flirted with the girls while vigorously reaching for the jug of cider, which they eagerly gulped down. Threshing wheat was one of the year's highlights for farmers.

My uncle, who was still single at the time, shared his ground-floor bedroom with me. Alois was always the first to get up at six in the morning to cut fresh grass for the cows in the meadows surrounding the house. He did this by sharpening the scythe with a longish whetstone and had to hammer it sharply from time to time;

the noise he made was more effective than any alarm clock in waking me up. Mowing with a scythe necessitates a unique swing; I was too young for it as a child, and I still couldn't do it as an adult. While Alois was feeding grass to the two cows and the oxen, the pigs discovered their first meal in the trough, which they had been waiting for, grunting loudly. Grandmother would start a fire with paper and wood shavings before adding larger logs. She served coffee, polenta, and farmer's bread with butter and honey to my uncle, Alois, herself, and I seated at the wooden table. She used the wood-burning cooker for both heating and cooking. A tank in the cooker's chimney provided hot water throughout the day. To control the temperature beneath the pans grandmother added or removed concentric metal rings from the hotplate with the aid of a wrought iron poker. As there were no other stoves in the house, we took hot water bottles to bed in the winter. She established the labor divisions in the house: emptying the ashes and scattering them in her vegetable garden or on the meadows every day was one of my domestic duties.

To draw fresh water we had to pull the side swivel of a water pump in the courtyard. Alois' craftsmanship was also essential in this case. Every two years, he disassembled the pump, cleaned a filter from the five-meter-deep shaft, and reassembled all the pieces. I kept an eye on him, handed him the parts, and assisted him with the assembly when he needed four hands to finish the task. Alois helped out in the stable and the fields. He tilled, sowed, harvested, and harrowed the land. Uncle would assist whenever he had time to spare.

On Saturday evenings, Alois made his regular visits to taverns in neighboring villages, where brawls and stabbings were common. On Sunday mornings he would emerge in his church clothes, bearing sores on his face and hands. These didn't worry him much, and he would already be looking forward to another brawl the following Saturday.

Alois went alone for Sunday morning service to Kumberg, where some of his family lived, but he never told me whom he visited. What about his parents, brothers, and sisters? Was he asked for lunch there, or did he eat at the local pub? He returned late in the afternoon with his knapsack full of sugar, yeast, salt, pepper, mustard, beer, sherbet powder and anything else Grandmother had requested.

Early on summer mornings, on days after the rain had fallen, Alois took me to pick mushrooms. He knew where they grew, a secret he kept from the neighbors, and entrusted only to me. I kept it, too; under no circumstances would I have let Alois down. As the sun rose, he showed me the chanterelles and half-hidden porcini under the leaves on the forest floor. He instructed me how to cut them with a pocket knife without damaging the more expansive underground plant tissue. I adored the aroma of the mushrooms I had picked. Taking a full basket to my grandmother's kitchen was one of life's simple pleasures. Alois often pretended I had found them because my eyes were closer to the ground.

Growing up on a farm, witnessing Alois slaughtering a pig two or three times a year was a regular event. He stunned the animal with a loaded bolt against its head, stabbed it in the throat, and collected the blood in tubs. I assisted in the collection and agitated the warm blood within three minutes to avoid clotting. With the help of my uncle, Alois would hang the animal upside down on the wall by the hind legs and begin to chop. The innards came first, then followed by the meat. Everything was edible apart from the intestines and bones. While he dissected the pig, he would place the warm heart, lungs, stomach, liver, and kidneys into my hands, explaining their function as he did so, and I would put them in buckets. Alois would marinade some bacon-like pieces of meat for two weeks in a herbal concoction before hanging them for several more to smoke in the chimney stack, accessible from under the roof. I admired Alois and wanted to be like him.

Herwig, this picture of my upbringing is still incomplete, at least until you hear about our forefathers.

MY ANCESTORS

As I've said, I considered my illegitimate beginnings to be a taboo subject for much of my life. As a result, neither you nor your siblings know our forefathers' past. I now wish to give you an insight into our family tree.

My great-grandfather, Matthäus Salmutter (1823-1905), a master tailor in Semriach, fathered seven children; he named his second youngest Valentin (1869-1903).

Valentin Salmutter stayed in Semriach and became a tailor like his father. He married my grandmother Amalia (1871-1951) when he was twenty-six – six weeks before giving birth to their daughter, my mother, whom they also baptized Amalia. In the five years following, my grandparents had five more children. Only Amalia (1895-1924) and Friedrich (1899-) reached adulthood; the rest died in infancy or childhood.

My mother Amalia was born at six in the morning, and immediately after lunch, at 2 pm, she was baptized. The thinking was, should she not survive, at least she would go to the kingdom of heaven! My mother spent her whole life in Semriach, where at the age of twenty-eight, unmarried, she died of a stomach ulcer.

My mother's occupation is not mentioned anywhere. She lived contentedly with my grandmother, who had lost her husband years earlier. My mother picked Valentin, her father's name, as my middle name.

**Extract from the marriage certificate
of Sepp Salmutter's grandfather, Valentin Salmutter,
written in the old German Kurrent script**

Grandmother Amalia outlived Valentin by another forty-eight years and after her daughter, my mother died in 1924 of her six children, only my uncle Friedrich remained alive.

My grandmother and uncle Friedrich were the only family members I knew after coming to Niederschöckl in 1926. I didn't know anything about my father's family, who he was, or anything of his background.

My grandmother and uncle Friedrich purchased the farm in equal parts. After she died, her share went to her son Friedrich. He sold the property and retired upon his 60th birthday in 1960. I had hoped for an inheritance, to be honest. On the other hand, my grandmother had disagreed with several of my decisions as a young man and had left the property to Friedrich. She had accepted my leaving the farm and attending the Franciscan seminary and grammar school, but my decision to quit the church and join the Waffen SS had been too much for her to bear.

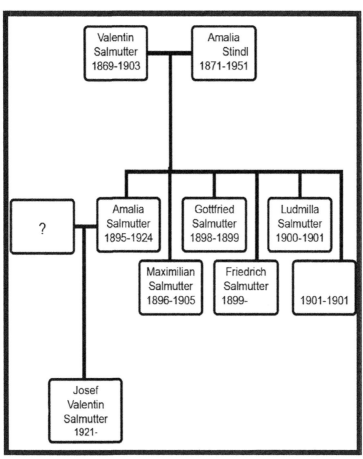

Family tree - Josef 'Sepp' Salmutter

FRANCISCAN SEMINARY, GRAZ

In Niederschöckl, I was an orphan with no siblings. Our catechist, who was also our parish priest, recognized my eagerness to learn and advised me to enroll in Graz's Franciscan seminary, which would enable me to attend the city grammar school. Grandmother half-heartedly agreed. Had I stayed on in the village and become a farmer, I would have inherited the farm as is tradition.

In 1931, carrying only a few belongings, I moved to Graz, where I remained a pupil at the seminary until 1938. The Franciscans bore all the expenses for food and accommodation.

At the seminary, life was different. The food, while not sumptuous, was palatable. At six o'clock in the morning, the superior roused us. A quick cat-lick with cold water and a light breakfast of warm broth followed. Was it tea or a coffee substitute we drank? Whatever it was, it tasted ghastly. The prayers were long and frequent. The Angelus was the day's first prayer after waking up and the last after dinner.

I was at the mercy of the seminary's strict rules and harsh punishments and though I reluctantly followed most of them, the monks often beat me. I put up with this for a while, but when I was twelve, things became unbearable. A young Franciscan fondled me several times and demanded I reciprocate. He told me to keep my mouth shut, but if I had protested, no one would have believed me.

Franciscan Church and Monastery, central Graz
Sepp Salmutter boarded here for seven years

Had I spoken up, the only consequence would have been another thrashing and possibly dismissal from the seminary. My resistance to the young Franciscan's advances was probably the only thing that saved me. He moved on to find another victim, who, if not eager, likely acted more like a stunned mouse. The monastery brothers imposed fear and subjection on us, but this was not my type of life, and I had no plans to become a clergyman.

SCHOOLBOY

In 1934, I had been in Graz for three years. As a Catholic seminarian, I shared a room with six youngsters my age. Older students attempted to bully us, but I learned how to stand my ground.

Graz opened up a whole new world to me with its well-planned streets and elegant architecture. The unpleasant odor emanating from horse droppings appeared less potent than in Niederschöckl; trucks, automobiles, the tramway and well-dressed women not wearing peasant headscarves made up the street scene.

I happily roamed alone through the streets and squares as I had no close friends at school. During my leisure time in the afternoons, I enjoyed the castle's double spiral staircase, the Painted House on Herrengasse Main Street, the numerous bridges over the river Mur, and the Mariahilf church in the Lend neighborhood on the other side of the river. I climbed Schlossberg Hill, either walking up past the French Cross or climbing the 260 War Steps. Sitting on a bench close to the Clock Tower, I would look down at the houses and streets of the Styrian capital. In front of me, I could make out the Town Hall and close by, my seminary with the tall tower of the Franciscan church. I counted sixteen church towers. They made me think about the war with the Turks 400 years ago when the Ottoman army had invaded central Europe. Miraculously they abandoned their siege of Graz in 1532, when Sultan Suleiman was urgently called back to Istanbul to fight the Persians. Had history taken a different turn, I might now be studying the Koran in a madrasa and admiring sixteen minarets from my vantage point.

Or I would practice my Latin vocabulary on the banks of the Mur, where I would think of the daring, wild river rafters who risked their lives to transport bundles of logs from the Alpine slopes down to Graz; of the Napoleonic army who blew up the Schlossberg castle in 1809 and of the inhabitants of Graz, who gathered gold ducats to give to the French soldiers and save both the bell and clock towers from destruction. I thought of Archduke Franz Ferdinand, born in a palace in the center of town and later slain in Sarajevo in 1914. Millions of innocent warriors would die on the battlefields of the subsequent First World War; that all began with the assassination of one of Graz's citizens.

Many students returned home to their families on Sundays, whereas I would grab a snack from the kitchen and ride my bike to Thalersee Lake for a swim, climb to the ruins of Gösting Castle, or else I would hike to the Gleinalm mountain meadows. I would explore local sights when the weather permitted, but during winter I always stayed in town. With no other responsibilities except passing my annual school examinations, my life was simple. One afternoon when I was ten, before sending me to the seminary, my sixty-year-old grandmother sat down with me at the dining table and explained,

> 'I am a Salmutter, your uncle Friedrich is a Salmutter, and you are a Salmutter. I wanted to avoid questions from curious villagers when we relocated from Semriach to Niederschöckl, six years ago, so I told them your mother and father had both

died young. Nothing out of the ordinary; at the time, people passed away like flies from the Spanish flu or other ailments. I had faintly pretended to be your father's mother, rather than your mother's mother. This ruse allowed me to explain your surname of Salmutter, and as a result, we were able to pass as a reputable family, unblemished in the villagers' eyes. Your mother is my daughter, and I have no idea who your father was.'

Until that point, I hadn't given much thought to my past. I soon discovered that my mother had sinned by falling pregnant with me without getting married in a Catholic church. An illegitimate child, however innocent, ranks low in the religious community's hierarchy, being the product of immoral activity, an unforgivable offense in God's eyes. My grandmother was a wise woman. She had wanted my mother's humiliation to be forgotten and had twisted the past to our advantage, without the need to hurt anyone else. I went along with my grandmother's narrative to avoid being bullied by my peers, hiding my illegitimacy from my closest confidants.

Although I was still young, I understood the need to keep certain secrets from others. I wasn't ashamed of my roots, but began to wonder if I ever would want to return to them or have anyone else know about them.

I didn't pay much attention to the Civil War, the 1934 putsch, or the subsequent political changes in Austria. People would converse reservedly behind closed doors. I would avoid street demonstrations for my own protection, as they invariably devolved into chaotic brawls.

Having matured noticeably in the past two years, I had now caught up with the rest of my class. At night, I dreamed about walking through the woods with a gorgeous girl dressed in a breezy, flowing summer dress. Her beautiful blonde curls tickled my cheeks as she got closer to me. When I woke up, I would be ashamed to discover that I had inadvertently stained my pajama bottoms. No one had taught me about the changes I would be going through. Neither my grandmother nor my uncle Friedrich ever revealed to me the 'facts of life.' I understood how rabbits bred and had seen a pig mount a sow, but I had no idea how humans did it. We learned the sixth commandment, 'Thou shalt not commit adultery,' but the catechist gave no further explanation during religious instruction.

Everything to do with sex was considered unchaste in the 1930s; one did not speak about it. Sex was something that was supposed to happen exclusively within a Christian marriage. Giving in to carnal inner desires constituted sacrilege. Subconsciously, I absorbed a sense of the church's power over me, requiring devotion to its rules and the conviction that failure to comply would result in tragedy. I was a devout Catholic who tried to please God and refrain from harboring sinful thoughts. My mind kept wandering, and during my dreaded weekly visits to the wood-carved confessional, I never mentioned my irrepressible desires.

In grammar school, I studied Greek and Latin. How were these old languages meant to aid me in mastering my destiny? Was I expected to become a village priest? Years would pass before I would need to decide on my life's path. Yet one thing was sure – though I was the sole heir,

I would not take over my grandmother's land. Farm life was grueling with long hours, and the weather was always a concern. If it rained in Graz, all you had to do was put up an umbrella. Whereas in Niederschöckl, Alois hastily had to recover the hay before spreading it out to dry again the next time the sun shone. Farmers lived in continual danger of hail damage, flooding, and the destruction of early or late frosts, as they still do today. Getting up at six in the morning to cut grass for cows was not part of the future I imagined. You couldn't go away for a few days as the cows needed milking, and all the animals required feeding. Since moving to Graz, I'd grown to adore the city's noise and activity, which I found liberating. I decided I'd rather drive a tram all day than plow, sow, or harvest crops.

Was I content during my time at the seminary? No. I liked a lot of things in grammar school. Greek was difficult for me, while Latin was one of my favorite topics. The latter's logic captivated me, and I believed a solid foundation would allow me to pursue a career in science. I wanted my dreams to become a reality. Learning and gaining excellent marks would be the first step towards not ending up as a farmer.

While in school, I encountered children from conventional families with a father, mother, and siblings. As an orphan from the age of four, I remember feeling like an outsider. Although I was not what you would call easygoing – more down to my personality rather than my being a parentless child – I would occasionally, but not frequently, receive an invitation. On those rare occasions, I would glimpse a different style of living, complete with servants, exquisite china, and spotless tablecloths. Most of my classmates played an instrument, but I didn't have the money or the interest to enroll in music classes or any other extracurricular activities.

What a surprise it must have been for the villagers in Niederschöckl, when on rare weekends I returned home to see my grandmother! Can you imagine being clean and well-groomed, well-dressed, and smelling like soap instead of stables? As a result, I had a lot of things to put up with back home. My pals, the peasant children, would mock me, saying, 'Haha, here comes the monk!' Eventually, after they had ceased to make fun of me, we all got along fine, and I became one of them again.

Grandmother made the greatest polenta, with an abundance of fruit and mushrooms. While replenishing our glasses with cider, she baked the porcinis like schnitzel and served the chanterelles with bread dumplings.

There was still a lot for me to learn, but at the age of thirteen, I realized nothing in life is ever perfect. On visits home, I saw that the village had its advantages: the simplicity of daily life, home-grown food, fresh rural air, and a close-knit community. In Graz, people treated one another as strangers, and despite the occasional beggar on the streets, there was a perpetual buzz of excitement. Both places had their positives and negatives. Similarly, whatever I chose to do in the future would have good or bad consequences.

Over the following years, I couldn't wait to become an adult and wondered when I might meet my first love.

*Clock tower on the Schlossberg in Graz, where Sepp learned
Latin vocabulary away from the noise of the city*

THERESIA

Herwig, for a long time, I debated whether to tell you about this period in my life. However, now that you're a grown-up, I've decided to write about Resi and the impact she's exerted on my life. She shaped me into who I am today. Had it not been for her, I might not have pursued medicine and followed a different path altogether.

To earn a bit of money, I gave private lessons to some of my younger peers. As a sixth-grade high school student, I tutored Karl, a third grade youngster. He, too, was a single child and lived with his parents in the heart of town – on Sporgasse Lane, where once a week I taught him Latin. Karl's family shared a traditionally furnished 19th-century flat with polished parquet flooring, ornamented walls, and richly decorated ceilings. He possessed his own room crammed full of toys. Though I was no longer a child, I was always envious of his possessions and can still recall his electric train with tracks running across half the room. As I had never owned such things to play with, this was pure luxury to me. Back at the farm, we used whatever was available to us: wood, iron wheels, stones, and glass marbles if we were lucky.

Karl's mother, Theresia Egger, would place money for the Latin lesson next to a cheese sandwich and a cup of tea each time I arrived. She was a cellist, while his father was a tax collector. After three months, when I was nearly seventeen, she asked if I could carry coal up from the cellar to the third floor for a friend who lived on Pestalozzi Street. She said her friend would pay the same rate I was getting for tutoring and I agreed.

Frau Egger was waiting for me in her friend's flat and greeted me warmly. I was surprised, but I'm not the type who asks many questions. After I had lugged up several crates of coal, she suggested I freshen up and rinse off the dust while she made us tea. When I got out of the shower, she stood in front of me, barefoot and clad in a short negligee. She put her arms around me and began kissing me then dragged me into the living room, pulled me down onto the couch, and held me close while loosening her underwear.

I fell into a kind of daze and, before I knew it, came all over her stomach, negligee, and couch, caught off guard by lust. I was at a loss for words. 'Never mind, young chap,' she responded with a smile. 'It was only to be expected.' Feeling humiliated I dressed as hurriedly as I could. 'Don't forget next week's Latin lesson with Karl!' she shouted after me as I walked out the door.

On the way home, I sat down on a bench in Augarten Park, my mind racing as I remembered the thorough-bred at the farm in Niederschöckl. The farmer had led him in a circle around the farmyard before dragging him onto a dummy board, upon which a farmhand had placed some furs. The stallion snorted through his nostrils without a mare in sight while the vet gathered his sperm in a glass. My friend Gerhard had said it was enough to inseminate ten mares artificially.

I continued to tutor Karl in Latin and once a week met Frau Egger at her friend's flat. She was an attractive brown-haired woman of medium height and frame, around 32 years old. As my self-control improved, I discovered what she liked and learned to be a more caring lover. She asked me to call her Resi, which felt strange at first. She would sometimes encourage me to speak vulgarly and act without inhibition, as she enjoyed role-playing with me as the master and her as the slave girl. I shed my shyness, and as I grew more confident as her partner, she begged me not to close the curtains, adding, 'Let's be honest, we have nothing to hide from each other.' After sex, she savored smoking a cigarette, but forbade me from doing the same.

Resi was the first person who genuinely cared about my future. My grandmother, uncle, teachers, and Franciscans – none had ever expressed an interest in my thoughts or outlook on life. She would inquire about my mother and grandmother, the primary school, and the farmers in Nieder-schöckl, as well as wanting to know how I got along with them all. She taught me how to respect others, that an ordinary man or woman could be a genius, and therefore I should never feel elitist or superior. Despite being a Catholic, Resi was unorthodox, despising the priesthood, and cautioned me against joining any religious order. She advised me to become an architect, a doctor, or an engineer saying it would not suit my personality to do a tedious, repetitive office job.

Resi's family was vital to her. She loved her husband and insisted her affair with me would not jeopardize her marriage.

House facade in the Sporgasse
Sepp gave private Latin lessons in one of these houses

Karl had a patient Latin instructor in me, and she was pleased when her son improved his grades.

She wanted to share new ideas with me, so our meetings were like weekly sermons moving and challenging me to think more critically. Later, as she got to know me, she confided in me about more serious topics, and I wondered if it was her ultimate purpose to prepare me for life. She suggested that without a modicum of self-control and setting myself limits, I would always be a restless spirit searching for stability, unable to find contentment.

Resi broadened my narrow worldview and showed me countless new perspectives: 'Stay out of the present anti-Jewish bigotry.' She adored Mendelssohn and Heine, and she enjoyed what the Nazis referred to as 'Negro music.' While listening to Benny Goodman or Big Bill Broonzy records, she stated, 'Nazi art can please but it is undemanding and folksy. Try to appreciate the cultures of the whole of Europe! You should try to read the Greeks and Shakespeare in their original languages. They, along with other Europeans like Rembrandt and Monteverdi, are our forefathers.'

Resi was a left-liberal intellectual who despised the Nazis in Germany. She felt people should live as individuals with fundamental human rights. She advised that in a dictatorship, you should at the least offer passive resistance. 'There is no need to act like a hero; no one has the right to expect it. You should study a variety of works, including those opposing your mindset.' She gave me Marx's Communist Manifesto, a small booklet published over a century earlier, and urged me to read Schopenhauer and Kant, as well as Nazi literature. She typed down the speech Pasteur gave on his 70th birthday, and I memorized it.

> 'Young men, young men, whatever your career may be,
> do not let yourselves become tainted
> by deprecating and barren skepticism,
> do not let yourselves be discouraged by the sadness
> of certain hours which pass over nations.
> Live in the serene peace of laboratories and libraries.
> Say to yourselves first:
> "What have I done for my instruction?"
> and, as you gradually advance,
> "What have I done for my country?"
> until the time comes when you may have
> the immense happiness of thinking that you have
> somehow contributed to the good of humanity.
> But whether our efforts are or are not favored by life,
> when we near life's end, let us be able to say,
> "I have done what I could."'

Resi's views on life differed from mine; she probed more profoundly, requiring more thinking than I had experienced in my school philosophy classes. I was madly in love with Resi, and I now know she was madly in love with me! She was a seductive, attentive, and concerned young mother who simply wanted the best for me. Whenever outdoors, I would address her politely and respectfully as Frau Egger. We conducted our relationship in secrecy, so as not to compromise her marriage. Thirty years have gone by, and I have never uttered a word about it to anyone. While other seminarians boasted of their conquests, I kept my mouth shut, partly for fear of being expelled from the seminary in disgrace.

Our romance lasted the best part of a year. At the start of my senior class in high school, Resi's friend relocated to Salzburg, which meant we could no longer continue with our secret rendezvous in her apartment. Meeting at Resi's place would have been far too dangerous. Also, I was kept busy preparing for my final exams and didn't have much time to spare.

Resi had become my mentor, and her influence had a far-reaching impact on the course of my life. I left the Catholic Church to pursue a career in medicine. Later, remembering what Resi had said to me, I deserted to the Americans. She will live on in my memory; a woman I will never forget.

ANSCHLUSS, 1938

If you ask today's Austrians what was the most important event in 1938, then whether they were alive at the time or not, they would tell you it was the Anschluss of Austria to Germany. You asked what had changed for me in March 1938, and, as is so often the case when you inquired about my past, you received no response. To be honest, I wasn't sure what to say. So much happened that I first had to figure out the sequence of events and their future ramifications for both myself and my hometown, before I could begin to write about it.

Austria had endured two catastrophic decades. Following the war defeat in 1918, the Habsburg monarchy was overthrown. The conquering powers reduced the multi-ethnic country to one-ninth of its original size, splitting off South Tyrol and Lower Styria. The 1919 Treaty of Saint-Germain imposed severe war reparations. From then until 1938, Austrians debated whether to remain a tiny independent nation or to join a Greater Germany. Hitler's invasion put a stop to the destabilizing indecision. Few could have predicted how the Anschluss would affect our lives, for better or worse.

Despite the difficulties, my grandmother, uncle, and I managed to make a decent living on the farm, whereas city folk were not so fortunate. After WWI, there was nothing – neither labor nor a well-functioning agricultural system – to ensure an adequate food supply. Mass graves were filled with a generation of young men. Many of the survivors were emotionally shattered and physically crippled upon returning home. The devastating Spanish flu subsequently killed many of those fortunate enough to have escaped the war. An icy spell caused widespread famine during the winters of 1918/19 and 1919/20. Many people thought Austria was no longer a functioning state, but the never-ending debate on joining Germany raged on. You see, the Anschluss was not a novel concept.

More than thirty years have passed since March 1938. Many political, social, or technological events may turn out to be watershed moments in a country's history, but they are only recognized as such in retrospect. Chancellor Engelbert Dollfuß outlawed the Social Democrats and National Socialist parties in 1934. Both organizations continued illegally and took their harmful activities underground. The illegal Austrian Nazis had considerable backing from the German motherland, and in the same year, Chancellor Dollfuß was assassinated in an abortive coup attempt. South Tyrolean Kurt Schuschnigg succeeded Dollfuß as head of state. He wished to maintain Austria's independence. Protests, demos, riots, and savage brawls in the streets between Socialists, Communists, and National Socialists were on the rise. There were casualties every week. Flag and torch marches were widespread, interspersed with Catholic processions.

Then in March 1938, after Austria became part of the German Reich, the brawls, the perpetual disorder, and all the disarray abruptly ended. Torchlight processions were the order of the day. Finally, it appeared as if the Nazis had determined Austria's fate.

IIA · 19356

The Führer Adolf Hitler on his parade ride through Graz,
the 'City of the People's Uprising', April 3, 1938

After March 1938, I didn't notice many people emigrating, but I did see many Germans immigrating to Austria. Many of my future SS colleagues and academic teachers from grammar school and the university had been members of the illegal German Nazi party long before 1938. A majority of Austrians who sympathized with the Nazis welcomed the Anschluss. The Nazis overthrew Chancellor Schuschnigg, who survived seven years of tyranny and abuse in a concentration camp.

Even among the most cynical observers, there was a distinct sense of hope and rejuvenation in the aftermath of the Anschluss. People had hoped for a more robust economy with higher pay and greater affluence. Furthermore, significant national objectives included returning to the world stage and regaining international respect. We knew that by the end of 1932, there were over five million unemployed Germans, and that within a few years, the Nazi dictatorship had brought about full employment. Many people in our country were impressed by this, and they sang Hitler's praises from the rooftops. Walserberg, near Salzburg, was the site of Austria's first German-built motorway. Within a year, war broke out, and the Nazis vowed to finish the road-building after their 'final victory.'

Germans appeared to be taking over senior positions, and everywhere I went, I heard heavy German accents. Many Austrians felt upset because we were no longer the sole rulers of our country. My grandmother, for one, despised the invading Germans. She thought they were arrogant and would push their worldview on us while doing nothing positive for the country. Her peasant wisdom proved correct.

In the days leading up to the Anschluss, Graz practically changed overnight. In February and March 1938, the streets were taken over by unlawful National Socialist demonstrations, with widespread flag-waving and rioting. Surprisingly, academics and students disproportionately supported the Nazi movement. On the occasion of a victory celebration on July 25, 1938, the Führer visited Graz, declaring our city would be given the honorary title 'City of People's Uprising' in recognition of its early support for National Socialism. Following the Anschluss, political opponents and Jews suffered relentlessly under Nazi terror. The Nuremberg Race Laws had an impact on about 2,400 Graz residents. They were persecuted and disenfranchised, and some were incarcerated in concentration camps.

Because I was only seventeen at the time, the Anschluss initially had little impact on my daily life. I had become a citizen of the German Third Reich without being asked but remained uninterested in ordinary politics. My life's primary interests were my grammar school and my affair with Resi. Like me, Resi was uninvolved in state affairs and was more concerned with justice and free expression. She disavowed Communism, National Socialism, and the Catholic Church. Our conversations were more intellectual, regarding truth, social behavior, equality, fraternity, the individual's position in society, and all other facets of culture. My understanding of present-day events was inadequate; only later did I realize what I hadn't grasped at the time. But even back in March 1938, however, I had a nagging sensation that something was amiss.

A sudden upheaval in my personal life was approaching: Catholic seminarians were about to be put through the wringer. After the Anschluss, our Styrian Gauleiter Uiber-reither, who despised Catholics, was influential in having the Franciscan seminary dissolved by state law. Religious orders suffered under the National Socialist dictatorship's new measures, which demanded the confiscation, abolition, or expropriation of all monasteries. Furthermore, the Nazis seized the opportunity for financial enrichment. The first house searches began in March 1938. Assets and properties were confiscated, and temporary administrators or trustees were appointed.

A decree concerning the church was issued, leaving it up to local school boards to assess whether preachers' lectures met the goals of National Socialist education. The bishop residing at the Catholic Cathedral, the Graz Dom, filed numerous complaints regarding Nazi harassment of monastic orders and church institutions, all to no avail. Nazis threatened religious communities by shutting down their educational and nursing programs, thus forcing the Elisabeth sisters to leave their convent in Graz in January 1939 and sell their hospital in Graz. The secret police force, the Gestapo, seized significant items of art belonging to the Elisabeth order and handed them over to the Graz Joanneum Museum.

After being forced to quit the seminary, I needed to find new housing, though only a few months of the school year remained before graduation. A Catholic family in Sackstrasse Street took pity on me and found a room in their attic. Soon after, I got a room in a student home. One thing was sure: I had no desire to return to the Nieder-schöckl farm.

Sports, rather than politics, were what captured my interest. Vienna hosted the European Football Cup, and as boys, we supported our side. However, due to German annexation, the event was canceled in April.

Rudolf Caracciola, the Silver Arrows' Mercedes racing driver, Rosemeier and von Brauchitsch were extremely popular. As an Austrian, my heart went out to Karl Gall, who got killed while riding his BMW motorcycle at the Isle of Man TT Races.

Mountaineers dubbed the Eiger North Face the 'killer rock face.' Climbers from many countries had died while attempting to ascend it. The successful first ascent by a German-Austrian foursome in 1938 thrilled me no end. You must be familiar with our legendary mountaineer Heinrich Harrer, who had studied at Graz a few years before me and spent seven years in Tibet as a teacher and friend of the Dalai Lama. The quartet included two German rock climbers, Ludwig Vörg and Anderl Heckmair, and the other Austrian was Fritz Kasparek.

Nazi propaganda used the Eiger success as a helpful tool, depicting it as a symbol of cooperation between Reichs-Germans and the 'new Germans' who had previously been Austrians. During a Berlin reception, the Führer took the opportunity to congratulate all four mountaineers on their brave endeavor and shook their hands in front of the cameras. When I watched this on a newsreel in the cinema a week later, I was moved to tears. Mountain sports were not my thing, but the bravery and talent demonstrated by these men made us all proud to be German.

GIRLFRIENDS AT SCHOOL

Some students fall in love for the first time while in high school. Others fall in love with numerous girls concurrently. I had been a diligent student, but I had no true friends and didn't belong to any cliques. Frankly, I was a loner. On an emotional level, personal contact with others was burdensome to me. My relationship with Resi had been straightforward since she had been so kind and understanding. There was no need to act or boast in front of her, because she accepted me for who I was. Unfortunately, in June 1938, my afternoons with Resi came to an end.

Despite being one of the better pupils in school, I lacked self-confidence. Some of my classmates perceived this as arrogance, which didn't bother me, and I remained aloof, hiding behind the mask of elitism. Nonetheless, I participated in bike rides and mountain walks including overnight stays in cabins. I met students from the girls' class, many of whom were intrigued by my solitary character and seemed eager to learn more about me. Although I was clever, decent-looking, and athletic, I had trouble chatting with girls. Some of them lived in the city's posh villa districts, and on occasion, I would receive an invitation to one of their birthday parties. They would take vacations with their families in Italy or Germany, and a family car often stood in their driveway. Their parents were curious about my background. I lied, saying my father was the business manager of a slaughterhouse in the village of Gratkorn and that I lived in the seminary, closer to the school. This narrative was not good enough for some, and my friendship with their daughters was discouraged.

Sunrise over Graz, view from the Schlossberg

Girls clung to me like burrs as we walked through town, possibly because of my shyness. To my dismay, none of these flirtations wound up in bed, as the dread of pregnancy was too great. They were put off, not so much by Catholic morals, as by the fear of losing their reputation. I had little respect for most of them, finding them dull. Our conversations, consisting mainly of gossip about fellow students, were anything but intelligent.

One hot summer day, I rode my bike with one of the girls to the outskirts of Graz, where we dismounted and walked into a meadow surrounded by woodland. We lay down in the grass, where she proceeded to pull down her panties and hang them over the handlebars, teasingly saying, 'I need a bit of ventilation. This humid jungle atmosphere is not conducive to my health.' She let me come close, but no further. I had hoped for more but was disappointed, and we returned home on our bikes. That was the end of it.

On a separate occasion, I invited another girl to the neighborhood movie theater. We fumbled around; she undid my trousers and went down on me. Later on, wiping me dry with her handkerchief, she whispered, 'I'll sniff my hankie tonight while pleasuring myself.' The next day in the schoolyard, she smiled but avoided me. I felt humiliated at the time: was I nothing more than a sex object? Was I going to be another trophy in her poetry book, marked 'Sepp' on a page headed 'Cinema' and a date?

In the winter, six months before the final exams, a fine-looking student approached me and asked if I might tutor her in Latin. She was afraid of failing her class. She shared the home with her mother, who worked in the afternoons. When we got to her apartment, she sat down on the couch, pulled up her jumper, exposed her firm breasts, and muttered, 'Kiss me.' I gladly obliged, and she began to moan and wriggle. I wanted more, but she refused, saying, 'No, please don't!' I never tried to impose myself on a girl, but I realized there was more to learn about understanding gestures and tones of voice, which I still found difficult. Though some girls desired sex as much as I did, they would pretend to put up a fight to maintain their dignity. The question was, who meant it, and who didn't?

In the end, I wasn't crazy about my female schoolmates. They were too capricious, self-centered, and liked to play cat-and-mouse. Why did it have to be so complicated? Perhaps nobody was to blame, but I knew none of them could ever match Resi. It was difficult for me to form any friendship or romantic relationship because I couldn't figure out other people's emotions and adequately express my own.

The end of high school was approaching. I sat down on the banks of the river Mur and mused what the future held, and how far I might be able to influence it.

GRADUATION YEAR, 1939

While sitting on a park bench high above town, next to the clock tower on Schlossberg Hill I practiced my Latin vocabulary and indulged in many a gloomy thought: I had no money, was not a member of a sports club, rarely went to the theater, couldn't play a musical instrument, and both mountain climbing and skiing were too expensive and time-consuming. Furthermore, the Nazis had closed down my seminary; I pursued no leisure activities and had lost contact with Resi. What did the future have in store for me? Would the new Nazi authorities decide my fate, or would I be allowed to choose it for myself?

Now, thirty years on, looking back, I can say, 'What on earth did I have to gripe about?' Granted, I had turned eighteen, and everything I knew was crumbling beneath my feet. I had been an orphan peasant child, now living in a large city without monetary and emotional support. Soon I would have a high school diploma in my pocket, but what would happen next?

I didn't have enough money to continue my education or travel abroad. I could have found work as a menial clerk or public servant, but this didn't appeal to me in the slightest, and I felt utterly insecure. Of course, most eighteen-year-olds undoubtedly feel that way, but back then I thought I was the only one suffering like that.

The high school ball, programmed for late January 1939, was one of the year's highlights. During October and

**Mariahilf Church in Graz,
view of the Koralpe mountains in the background**

November, I took dance classes in the Geidorf neighborhood and became a competent ballroom dancer. I enjoyed it, as there was no need for me to make small talk with any one of my partners; all I had to do was guide them whilst holding them close. However, when I went to a ball in Graz's poorer Lend district, on the other side of the Mur, I found it impossible trying to keep up with the young working-class lads' wit, which tended to dampen my mood.

In June 1939, I graduated from the Graz school, where I had finished near the top of my class, making me eligible to attend university. Throughout my eight years at grammar school, I enjoyed learning and excelled at sport competitions, both of which had become priorities on the Nazi agenda.

The Nazis had ushered in a new era. Swastikas adorned buildings, and uniformed soldiers saluted on the streets. German order and thoroughness defined our lives. No longer a country, Austria was now a German region named Ostmark.

I was alone, with no one in whom I could confide and no one to give me advice. For a long time, anatomy had interested me, and it had been my ambition to pursue a career in medicine. Intellectually, there would be no issue for me but I couldn't say the same about the cost of my studies, because I was broke. With this in mind, I started looking for strategies to achieve my aim. Dalliances with girls and casual pastimes could wait – now was the moment to define my destiny. I was approaching a watershed moment in my life.

The interrogating Americans at Fort Hunt became interested in my story from this point forward. Understanding the reasons for one's actions can be challenging at a given moment, let alone years later; no matter what I decided, I had no idea where it would lead me. All I had to go on was what Resi had warned me of: a pointless administrative position buried away in some dingy office would be the end of me. I agreed.

JOINING THE WAFFEN SS

Herwig, before you pass judgment on my decisions, try to imagine yourself in my shoes. A year before, the Anschluss had occurred. The Nazis were beginning to gain a foothold in all aspects of life. At the age of eighteen, it is impossible to see the big picture and fully comprehend the political situation of the day. It is much easier to appraise past events with the benefit of hindsight. At the time, I could only deal with the unfolding present.

A new opportunity came to my rescue:

> *'SS Hauptsturmführer Rinech of the 2nd Battalion 'Der Führer,' a doctor stationed in Graz-Wetzelsdorf whose son I had met at school, drew my attention to the SS Medical Academy scheduled to be opened in Graz. It would be possible to study during the war for the training of troop doctors, provided one gained front-line experience as a member of an SS unit.' [Curriculum vitae]*

The Waffen SS would pay for my studies. I had believed in the concept of the New German citizen – one who was honest, loyal, ambitious, and moral. As a result, joining the Waffen SS, which claimed to possess all of these attributes, did not appear to be a significant step. Years later, I would realize that the SS had duped me.

You could say that joining the Waffen SS was a pact with the devil, albeit made in adolescent ignorance. The Waffen SS promised to fund my studies, allowing me to obtain a medical degree and work as a respected and well-paid professional doctor! I would have a secure place of residence during my studies, a soldier's wages, and a dazzling black uniform.

Nazi Propaganda SS Recruitment poster
'Enrollment form age 17'

All I had to do in return was a little front line war service. What was the problem? Upon reflection, I wish I had read Goethe's Faust!

I had set aside Resi's doubts about the National Socialist doctrine. It wasn't until the tail end of the war, when I saw her again, that I understood her opposition to authoritarianism, Nazi control, and the Waffen SS. I will come back to this later.

In October 1939, I had no reservations about leaving the Catholic Church, as by then I had lost my Christian faith. At the seminary, I had witnessed abusive events and was subjected to a clergyman's advances first hand. It prompted me to inquire, 'In which eye was the good Lord blind?' How could God, if he existed, overlook such heinous behavior? My departure from the church was not difficult, and Resi would not have scolded me, though she might have questioned my motives, to see if I had thought things through. Regrettably, we were no longer in each other's lives. There were devoted, self-sacrificing, spiritual Catholic pastors who sought to persuade me not to take such an extreme action, but even the clergy admitted that, by 1938, times had changed.

Siegfried Uiberreither, the provincial political leader of Styria, was one of the church's sharpest opponents, seeing Catholicism as a disruptive force in the Nazis' totalitarian claim to power. He casually spoke to me at SS gatherings on multiple occasions, though I never had to interact with him in any formal capacity.

> 'He [Uiberreither] was an SA brigade leader and lawyer, Gauleiter and Reichsstatthalter of Styria. Party member before the Anschluss. Resided in Graz. Medium height, dark complexion, narrow face, saber wounds on the cheek. SA leader in Styria before the Anschluss. Fanatical follower of Hitler. Hated by the people of Styria.' [questionnaire]

I presented my above statement to be added to his US records. In May 1945, after the Allies had occupied the German Reich and Hitler had shot himself, they arrested Uiberreither. He testified as a witness at the Nuremberg Trials. In 1947, he managed to escape to Argentina to avoid being handed over to Yugoslavia, where he was accused of being a war criminal and where he would have faced a war crime prosecution. Later in life, he lived with his family in Sindelfingen, near Stuttgart, using an alias, thus evading prosecution for Nazi crimes.

My grandmother railed against my quitting the Catholic Church and repeatedly chastised me for it. Like the majority of rural people, she attended Sunday services. The church still wielded enormous influence and authority over the lives of the faithful. She refused to accept my having joined the SS to study medicine at the SS Medical Academy, sensing the enticing power of the National Socialists, including the Waffen SS. It was the straw that broke the camel's back. Despite exchanging harsh words with her, I did not change my opinion or decision on either count.

My Latin teacher became the third individual to try and persuade me not to join the Waffen SS. He reminded me of the writings of Heine in one of his critical essays, which we translated into Latin. 'Heine is a Jew, someone to look up to. Remember, Sepp.'

The SS, an establishment holding its own worldview, noted my drifting away from the church with satisfaction. In the years to come, Himmler would give the SS a pseudo-religious character with magnificent rites and impressive symbolism, stylizing them as modern crusaders in the conquest of Aryanism. Torches, flags and marches replaced candles and incense.

I envisaged the SS as a fearless, morally and ideologically untouchable band of young men. I bore no sense of imminent disaster. Although I did not believe everything they said, I agreed with their ideas on elitism. Only after the war did I learn the truth.

Reichsführer SS Heinrich Himmler founded the Waffen SS after the invasion of Poland in December 1939, by combining several SS Divisions. The earliest Division consisted of 120 troops from a barracked Special Squad in 1934. Their first mission was to safeguard higherranking SS and Nazi party leaders. They participated in raids and the arrests of political opponents, whom they imprisoned. From 1940 until 1945, the Waffen SS grew into a separate military organization with 900,000 men. The 2nd SS Panzer Division 'Das Reich,' in which I served as a medic, was founded in 1940 and initially only volunteers signed up to it.

In the summer of 1940, the Führer placed the SS directly under the supreme command of Himmler. It included combat forces, as well as concentration camp guards. Units of the Waffen SS fought on the front lines, secured conquered territory, and committed numerous war crimes.

Following the unsuccessful assassination attempt on Adolf Hitler's life on July 20, 1944, in which officers of the army – the Wehrmacht – took part, the Führer gave the Waffen SS extra powers formerly held by the Wehrmacht.

Nazi propaganda portrayed members of the Waffen SS as elite warriors with an aura of invincibility, distinguished by their unrivaled ferocity and cruelty. They described themselves as a force whose members were virile, courageous, fearless, steadfastly devoted and self-sacrificing, and they boasted of being merciless towards partisans fighting German forces.

In 1934 and 1935, the SS established military SS Junker Schools in Tölz and Braunschweig to train SS leaders. In 1941 and 1942, I served as a trainee at both institutions. Heinrich Himmler, head of the SS, intended to create fully-fledged military Divisions swearing total loyalty to Adolf Hitler and to be available at his command.

Following National Socialist philosophy, the SS evolved into a racial and political leadership class. Belief in the Führer, Aryan supremacy, unquestioning loyalty, and willingness to self-sacrifice were all mandatory and instilled into the recruits from day one at military school. An SS member had to be ruthless enough to slit a child's throat if the situation demanded; we were trained for such brutal operations like Rottweiler dogs. Strong emphasis was laid on camaraderie. Private belongings were not locked up, mutual trust was assumed, and stealing from a comrade could result in execution. Members of the Waffen SS were taught to think and act as a unit and permitted themselves to be led into acts of cruelty and murder they would not have carried out as individuals.

The SS consisted of the Waffen SS Panzer Divisions on one side, and the SS Death's Head Divisions operating in concentration and extermination camps on the other. After the war, the victors should not have viewed the military Waffen SS in the same way as the SS Divisions in charge of the camps. During the Nuremberg trials, postwar politicians made things simpler for themselves by declaring the Waffen SS a criminal organization as a whole, regardless of the roles, duties, deeds, and faults of individual members within the various Divisions. As a result, I was labeled a criminal despite serving exclusively at the front in an SS Panzer Division, never in camps.

The SS established a Research Institute in 1942, which conducted deadly and barbaric experiments on detainees in Nazi concentration camps. At the Nuremberg Medical Trial, a mere twenty of the 3,000 camp doctors and three others were proven guilty and some of those so-called scientists were Waffen SS members.

Members of the Waffen SS had their blood group tattooed on the inside of their left upper arms, a vital identifying mark helping the Allies distinguish civilians and Wehrmacht soldiers from Waffen SS members, both during and after the war. To this day, I never had this tattoo removed, I do not have to apologize for any crimes.

In the early years of the war, the Waffen SS lacked trained officers. My Division was not engaged in actual fighting in

France at the start of the war in 1940, and officers' bravado did not expose me to any unnecessary danger. In later years, the SS military leadership improved their tactics. By the time I fought in the Battle of the Bulge in 1944 in the snow-covered Ardennes forests, our superiors had become experienced war tacticians

The most tenacious, dependable, and loyal SS Panzer Divisions were:

1st SS Panzer Division Leibstandarte SS Adolf Hitler
2nd SS Panzer Division Das Reich
3rd SS Panzer Division Totenkopf
9th SS Panzer Division Hohenstaufen
12th SS Panzer Division Hitler Youth

SS MEDICAL ACADEMY, 1ST TRIMESTER

After joining the Waffen SS and completing eight weeks of basic military training, in December 1939, I enrolled for the first trimester at the Karl Franzens University in Graz.

I lived at the newly established SS Medical Academy in Graz and was promoted to Unterscharführer – the equivalent of a corporal in the UK. The Academy's mission was to shape its members into the ideal blend of political soldiers and medical professionals. Discipline was severe, and superiors punished even minimal violations.

> 'I was a student and officer at the same time. It never suited me. They constantly harassed us. Running around naked outside and all that nonsense. That's how I got my kidney and bladder disease.' [eavesdropped]

For the actual study of medicine, I attended regular courses at the university such as anatomy, physics, chemistry, and the history of medicine and a freshly launched university subject – Heredity and Race Studies with Professor Dr. Alfred Pischinger.

All lectures demanded my complete attention and required significantly more effort than my earlier education. I took part in science workshops and in a dissection course. I enjoyed my studies, though they only lasted three months, until March 1940, when the SS ordered me to attend military training, followed by deployment to the front.

Morning roll call
The discipline at the SS Medical Academy was harsch

The Waffen SS requested that I serve at the front and become a troop doctor in order to qualify and join the medical profession. This was the deal I had made. I was pleased with my life, and it wasn't as horrible as Resi, my Latin teacher, and my grandmother had predicted. At least, not yet.

GUNNER WEAPONS TRAINING

From February to May 1940, after a short, but stimulating period of university study, I was called up for weapons training as a gunner attached to the 2nd Artillery Replacement Detachment in Berlin-Lichterfelde.

> *'Basic training with 2./SS Art. Ers. Abt. in Berlin/Lichterfelde. Training as gunner.' [Curriculum vitae]*

As with other soldiers drafted there, I had intensive military training, including trekking long distances in uniform while wearing heavy boots and carrying an assault rifle. Furthermore, we were exposed to constant harassment to instill obedience and discipline. After exercise, our officers severely restricted our movements, and we were confined to the barracks.

We slept five to a room. My closest comrades were ordinary young guys aged 17 to 19, from all across the Reich, and none had a high school diploma. My education was superior to theirs, but I didn't show it. Over time, we grew to rely on one other, whether in personal matters or when completing military activities. We fulfilled a stringent regimen, getting up at six and starting artillery training straight after breakfast. Lessons concentrated on practice, with little emphasis on artillery theory.

The days passed without incident, and in the evenings, once we had eaten and washed, we talked shop before retiring to bed. Of course, we also gossiped and ranted about women. I wasn't sure if some of my comrades had ever had sexual encounters. Whatever, the important thing was we had a good time, sharing our adventures – real or imagined.

Artillery is a necessary component of ground forces. Its mission is to destroy installations as well as hostile guns. I trained on the IG18 light 7.5 cm infantry gun; Rheinmetall designed it in 1927 and produced over 12,000 units between 1932 and 1945. They weighed 400 kg, were beautifully balanced, and moved on two wooden spoke wheels akin to an ox cart, with independently sprung springs. Five gunners, four on the draw bar and one pushing from behind, could drag it into position on hard ground. We moved the gun either by horse or by tethering it to a motor vehicle for long distances. The barrel measured slightly under a meter in length. Gunners could fire up to twelve projectiles per minute over a three-and-a-half-kilometer range if they worked well together. Of course, we shielded our ears from the blast, but I'll admit to enjoying the sounds and smells of the explosions.

The IG18 gun was a part of light infantry and rifle regiments and later part of heavy infantry companies, SS armored infantry battalions, and the Wehrmacht. Its range was short, but it produced satisfactory field results and proved reliable. Despite the undersized barrel, the army could use it at distances of up to 300 meters directed against lightly armored targets, such as reconnaissance vehicles, by firing explosive grenades. We practiced with grenades which could penetrate up to 8 centimeters of thick armored steel, sufficient to put close-by medium-sized tanks out of action.

In our five-man gunnery team, we each performed our assigned tasks – positioning the six-kilogram projectile

Infantry gun IG-18
Sepp Salmutter had been ordered to undergo training in
Berlin-Lichterfelde, 1940

next to the gun, loading it, firing it, and removing the hot cartridge. This entire process went without a hitch by the end of the training. We used split ammo and transported the projectile and propellant charges separately, assembling them before loading. Five rings made up the explosive charge. We could use all five or fewer for closer targets depending on how far we wanted to shoot. We achieved a firing rate of 8-10 shots per minute during basic artillery training.

In real front line action, we would observe the impact of our projectiles and reset the gun to the target. A forward observer would determine the point of hit with a scissor-telescope and instruct us via field telephone to readjust the cannon.

We had to prepare for possible injuries or personnel failure; therefore, each team member had learned how to operate in all the positions. We were taught how to disassemble, repair, and maintain the gun and how to make quick position changes, whether in daylight or complete darkness of night. In an emergency, moving speedily was vital for survival because once we had fired our projectiles, the enemy would know our location. Tactics, reading maps, and calculating trajectories with the help of firing tables were all part of the training.

No matter where you served – whether with the ground troops, in tanks, or high in the air – the possibility of death was ever-present. Like all soldiers everywhere and throughout history, we just hoped for the best.

FRENCH CAMPAIGN, 1940

From June to September 1940, I experienced my first front duty, serving in the 2nd SS Panzer Division Das Reich, after finishing gunnery training in Lichterfelde.

> *'Front line service (Frontbewährung) in France with 13./SS Art. Regt., a basic artillery unit that did not see action.'*
> [Curriculum vitae]

As part of the Western campaign, the Division served in France, the Netherlands, and Belgium beginning in May 1940. We battled alongside units from the SS Leibstandarte Adolf Hitler and SS Totenkopf Divisions.

Despite being trained as a gunner, I served in the medical corps as Unterscharführer and could not put my gunner training to effective use. That was fine with me, as I preferred serving as a medic. Furthermore, in the summer of 1940, we fought no battles, our campaign required neither heavy nor light artillery, so I would have been no less safe as a gunner than as a medic.

In a glorious summer, we advanced from southern France to Holland. Being abroad for the first time in my life almost felt like being on a paid holiday. I barely noticed the war. It was nothing like grandmother had foretold, so I concluded that I hadn't been so foolish after all, and for now, my pact with the devil held.

I spent six weeks in Amersfoort, near Utrecht in the Netherlands, at the end of the campaign. German forces had controlled the Dutch territory since May.

'Occupation of the Netherlands near Amersfoort.'
[Curriculum vitae]

We spent a great time amongst ourselves. My German comrades referred to me as 'Ostmärker' and 'Kamerad bootlaces,' indicating a gentle mockery of Austrians, a feature of the German attitude since the First World War.

In the late summer of 1940, I hoped for long-term peace in Europe. We had conquered Poland a year before. The French campaign began in early May, during my gunnery training, and by the end of June, we had beaten France and pushed the English back home at Dunkirk. We expected the political and military situation to stabilize in June, and everything appeared to look okay. I genuinely hoped I would soon be able to resume my medical studies in peace.

SS-Unterscharführer Sepp Salmutter, 1940
First frontline experience in France as a paramedic
in the 2nd SS Panzer Division 'Das Reich'

SS MEDICAL ACADEMY, 2ND TRIMESTER

After the French campaign, the SS allowed me to return to Graz to study for three months, from October to December 1940. My former classmates were a year ahead of me in the university's curriculum, but they lagged far behind in terms of life experience; they had lived securely and known nothing about life at the front. I impressed female students by portraying myself as a rugged and brave daredevil, complete with tales from the service at the front – greatly embellished, of course.

Academic courses were similar to those in the first trimester: Anatomy Part II with Prof. Dr. Hafferl, Physics with Prof. Dr. Rumpf, Chemistry with Prof. Dr. Lieb, Zoology and Botany, and Histology with Prof. Dr. Meixner. In addition, part of my studies involved excursions around the vicinity of Graz identifying medicinal herbs.

If you're curious, Herwig, I'll tell you about my professors, to whom I owe so much. I idolized many of my instructors and looked up to them with reverence and admiration. Nearly all held a National Socialist viewpoint, with which they effortlessly indoctrinated their young pupils. We didn't know anything else. All sources of political information, news, and newspapers led us in the same direction. Without us noticing, our brains were subtly washed, drop by drop: National Socialism was the future. They cast their net, and I got caught in it.

Professor Dr. Anton Hafferl taught anatomy. He had a slim physique, a high forehead and a thick mustache that made his face very striking. Professor Hafferl was one of the most significant members of the Viennese Anatomical School, he published critical scientific articles, and had prepared an anatomy textbook. From 1933 to 1959, he was the Graz University Anatomical Institute's director, and his students revered him. Anatomy became one of my favorite courses, and Prof. Hafferl one of my favorite lecturers, I would always arrive early in the lecture hall, anticipating his entrance.

Professor Hafferl introduced new students to anatomy and general medicine as a prerequisite to becoming a doctor. He reminded us to be conscious of the high level of responsibility coming with this job. He did not tolerate carelessness or a lack of knowledge. Mistakes would cause irreversible damage and, in the worst-case scenario, the death of a patient. We pored over the positions of muscles and nerves, studied the outlines of bones with all their appendages and depressions, and navigated the fleshy passageways of the brain in the laboratory like geographers do with maps. He expected his students to apply the highest standards and reminded us of our societal responsibilities. In the dissecting room, the professor asked us to respect the human body parts we dissected and to remember that these body components had come from people who had once been alive. After the war we discovered the origin of those human parts. More about this later.

The university's Medical Faculty was rife with dedicated Nazis and Nazi supporters. The Nazi German Lecturers' Association played a vital role in the expulsion of Jewish academics from universities. Aside from Party doctrine, the racial issue became prominent in higher education.

Prof. Hafferl became chairman of the Nazi Lecturers' Association following Austria's annexation in 1938. He knew Styrian Gauleiter Siegfried Uiberreither and the dean of my SS Medical Academy, SS Sturmbannführer Bernward Gottlieb.

I studied Physics I and II with Prof. Dr. Erich Rumpf in the first and second trimesters. At the start of each lecture, he demanded all students to rise and give the Heil Hitler salute with outstretched arms. Aside from this non-academic behavior, I found Prof. Rumpf to be approachable and helpful to all freshmen at the university.

During my first four semesters, Prof. Dr. Hans Lieb taught Chemistry I and II, Physiological Chemistry, Chemistry of Warfare Agents, and the Physiological-Chemical Practical Course. He was pleasant, despite his introversion. He wrote the formulae for long hydrocarbon compounds on the enormous chalkboard at breakneck speed, and I remember overhearing a fellow student next to me moan, 'Now I give up!' Professor Lieb did not lack patience with students, but he was preoccupied with his research. He had been a student and colleague of Graz Nobel Prize winner Fritz Pregl, who had played an essential role in developing the micro-analysis of chemical substances. Prof. Lieb's admiration for Fritz Pregl was evident whenever he mentioned the man's name.

Prof. Lieb remained a sought after specialist on the deadly gases which blinded First World War soldiers. During the Second World War, he created noxious and toxic gases for military use. After the war, the British occupation forces put Prof. Lieb on trial, and only his recognized scientific

Semester 1 and 2	
Anatomy I + II	Hafferl
Physics I + II	Hull
Chemistry I + II	Lieb
Chemical Practical Course	Lieb
Heredity and Race Studies	Pischinger
Histology	Pischinger
Zoology	Meixner
Botany	Weber
Medicinal herb excursions	N. N.
History of Medicine	Moro
Physics practical course	Rumpf
3rd and 4th semester	
Physiology I + II	Löhner
Physiological practical course	Löhner
Anatomy III	Hafferl
Taxidermy Course I + II	Hafferl
Embryology	Pischinger
Histological-Microscopic Course	Pischinger
Microscopic Anatomy	Pischinger
Population policy	Polland
Physiological Chemistry	Lieb
Chemistry of Warfare Agents	Lieb
Physiological-Chemical Practical Course	Lieb
Occupational and Defence Physiology	N.N.
Semester 5	
Medical Clinic	Hoff
Obstetrics and gynaecology course	Hoff
Surgical Clinic	Winkelbauer
Special Pathological Anatomy	Feyter
Pharmaceutical and Toxicology I	Flower
Percussion and auscultation	Schnetz
Hygiene	Schmidt-Lange
Bacteriological - serological course	Schmidt-Lange
Topographical Anatomy	Hafferl
Semester 6	
Surgical propaedeutics	Winkelbauer
Obstetrics Propaedeutics	Hoff
Pathology and defence pathology	Feyter
Clinical Chemistry Course	Schrade
Medical Propaedeutics	Schnetz
Medical Radiology	Leb
Pharmaceutical and Toxicology II	Blume

Salmutter's curriculum at Graz University, 1st to 6th semester

expertise kept him from being prosecuted for war crimes. In early 1945, not knowing what I know now, I ranked Prof. Dr. Lieb among the anti-Nazis:

> *'Prof. Dr. Hans Lieb, university professor for medicinal chemistry, Graz, Bergmanngasse 24, Christian- socialist, Roman Catholic (very keen Catholic, churchgoer despite hostility from Nazis).' [questionnaire]*

I studied Histology and Embryology with Professor Dr. Alfred Pischinger for my first four terms and enrolled in his Practical Histological Microscopy course. Many first-year students considered his lectures easygoing, informal and taught lightheartedly

I enjoyed learning how to evaluate and draw a microscopic image. The institute's atmosphere felt life-affirming and uplifting thus inspiring a thirst and zeal to study. We kept up with his most recent scientific findings on the nature of cells and cell nuclei, which he explained in his notable Austrian dialect. He was recognized for his contributions to coloring methods and was the first to precisely record the physical-chemical processes in histological staining techniques. He is regarded as the father of histo-chemistry.

In the first trimester, I attended Prof. Pischinger's lecture on 'Heredity and Racial Science,' a classic National Socialist subject. He had become a specialist in the field known as 'racial hygiene.' Thus, it was unsurprising to hear later he had been an illegal member of the Nazi Party in the early days and that he had joined the Storm Troopers after March 1938. The Nuremberg Race Laws strengthened National Socialist racial hygiene — an extreme version of eugenics. When I married, my future wife would be subject to those same Nazi racial laws.

SS MILITARY ACADEMY, TÖLZ

As soon as I finished my second trimester, the SS ordered me to attend their officers' school, the SS Military Academy, named 'Junker School' in Tölz, Bavaria, from February to March 1941. SS Junker Schools were military institutions training future military leaders for the Waffen SS. In addition to military training, they taught table manners, etiquette, and deportment consistent with an SS officer's stature in society. SS Junker Schools were all part of Reichs-führer SS Heinrich Himmler's military elitism.

> *Himmler's order was: Every Waffen SS troop doctor must complete an SS officers' academy training course.' [Curriculum vitae]*

In the autumn of 1936, Adolf Hitler inaugurated the first Junker School for SS officers in Tölz, and a second SS Junker School opened in Braunschweig in the summer of 1937.

Tactics, terrain and map studies, combat and weapons training, weapons technology, firing practice, drill, ideo-logical education, Waffen SS organization, physical training, communication and Intelligence training, practical motor vehicle training, basic tank training, basic Air Force training, and essential medical services were all part of our study plan at both Junker Schools.

The education of future SS officers would consist of half military and half ideological training. Our lecturers taught Aryan race studies and the core ideas of the so-called Greater German 'living space' philosophy alongside Germanic history; the former, of course, consisted of bringing significant sections of Eastern Europe under German domination. The National Socialist ideology pervaded all topics, including sports and athleticism, designed to imbue a spirit of aggression.

The SS Junker Schools chose their students, known as SS Junkers, on racial characteristics. The Academy only admitted those under twenty-four, at least 1.72 m tall and with perfect vision. A 'Great Aryan' certificate, tracing one's ancestors back to the 18th century was required, as well as a medical health record. Because I knew nothing about my father, I was granted exemption from my paternal lineage. My maternal relatives had lived in the tiny village of Semriach for generations, so it seemed unlikely my father would have been non-Aryan. The idea of a stranger wandering into this small and distant community long enough to get my mother pregnant was dismissed as implausible.

Aside from one's physical condition, no other skills were required. Thus, most Junker School recruits possessed only an elementary school diploma. Officers of the Waffen SS represented a racial, but not an intellectual elite. For this reason, our SS Junker institutions cannot be compared to prestigious officer schools such as the United States Military Academy at West Point or the British Royal Military Academy at Sandhurst, where a high school diploma was, and still is the minimum requirement.

While the Academy taught technical subjects of a high standard, ideological topics like racial studies and Nazi

**March through the main gate,
SS Officers' Military academy in Tölz, 1941**

ideology were less intellectually challenging. I saw through the Nazi propaganda, but remained silent to avoid offending my superiors.

It was a privilege to get accepted into one of the SS Junker Schools, and we consequently felt like top-tier soldiers. As it had been in the past for the Kaiser, the SS required loyalty to Hitler as well as hygiene, comradeship, athletics, short haircuts, and being able to fit into the SS brotherhood. I thought these requirements to be small-minded, specifically ordering us to give up all individuality. In my perspective, this was comradeship taken too far.

> *'Well, I might have been good in the mountain infantry, but the SS, that didn't suit me at all.'* [eavesdropped]

As a result, perhaps, my final Junker School report read:

> *'not suitable in character to be an SS leader.'* [Curriculum vitae]

Eventually, I was fired from the Military Academy in Tölz. However, during my time there, I was ordered to visit the Dachau concentration camp for three days.

> *'Only the good was shown there [Dachau].'* [eavesdropped]

At the Dachau camp, the Commander encouraged me to take a permanent post to conduct scientific research on prisoners for the advancement of medical science. I could have averted a potentially lethal deployment to the front lines if I had agreed. I was tempted to believe the research claims would be beneficial, but the camp Commander failed to persuade me and I felt the doctors there were breaking the Hippocratic Oath, so I responded by telling the camp director, 'Interesting, but no thanks.' I had no idea what horrific experiments the camp doctors were conducting at the time; all I knew was that using convicts for research was unethical, as their participation could not be assumed to be voluntary.

SS Junkers had to swear an oath to Adolf Hitler:

> I swear to you, Adolf Hitler,
> leader and chancellor of the German Reich,
> Loyalty and bravery.
> I pledge to you and your nominated superiors
> Obedience unto death!
> So help me God!

SS MILITARY SCHOOL, LAUENBURG

Despite having been promoted to the NCO grade of Unterscharführer in September 1940, I was sent by the SS to the NCO military school in Lauenburg from May to August 1941 for extensive army training. I enjoyed traveling, so I was delighted to get to know the German Reich from north to south and east to west. There are no mountains around Lauenburg in Western Pomerania, but many lakes had developed in the last Ice Age. During the sweltering summer of 1941, I frequently went swimming with my comrades – young men of my age from throughout the Reich. We had a wonderful time.

After Lauenburg, the SS transferred me to Oranienburg for troop paramedic training in September and October 1941. There I served as an Unterscharführer in the SS Medical Auxiliary Section. Again, I was forced to visit a concentration camp, for four days, this time Sachsenhausen-Oranienburg, north of Berlin.

> *Salmutter is a knowledgeable med. officer - intelligent. Cooperative , can be used for many purposes - Furnished extensive report on KZ "Oranienburg", "Very reliable". [office correspondence]*

Once more, the Camp Commandant approached me with an offer to serve as a doctor, which again I turned down. I preferred being a soldier at the front rather than working in a concentration camp.

**Sepp Salmutter enjoyed a hot and peaceful summer
at the surrounding lakes at the SS NCO military school
in Lauenburg, East Prussia, 1941**

SS MILITARY ACADEMY, BRAUNSCHWEIG

It was in the middle of the war, and while the general populace lacked many things, the military did not. I moved from one military school to another at the expense of the Reich. After my time in Lichterfelde, Tölz, Lauenburg, and Oranienburg, from November 1941 to April 1942, I attended the SS Junker School at the medieval Castle Square, in the charming old town of Braunschweig. My religious upbringing had taught me obedience and never to question authority – skills useful under the Nazi regime. I learned to fake enthusiasm, show reverence for National Socialism, and adhere to close comradeship codes; thus, I completed the officer training on April 2, 1942, with my report stating:

> *'Suitable for SS leadership in the medical service. '*
> *[Curriculum vitae]*

At the age of twenty-one, after more than a year of training, I finally became an SS officer. Further promotions to SS Standartenjunker came in February 1942, and to SS Standartenoberjunker in April.

A two-day excursion to the Buchenwald concentration camp near Weimar was part of the training at the Braunschweig Military Academy. It was the third concentration camp the SS had ordered me to visit, and I wasn't surprised when they invited me to take a permanent post as a doctor in a unit where, once again, they claimed to be conducting 'important research'. Once more, I declined.

Graduation medal of the SS Military Academy
(Junker Schule) at Braunschweig
Sepp Salmutter promoted to SS-Standartenoberjunker

They had shown me a clean, peaceful, well-equipped unit staffed by medical professionals. But I gained the impression something was wrong. I rationalized that instinctive reaction, by telling myself that a caring role as a doctor was at odds with research on incarcerated humans. I can't say I saw anything 'wrong' in the camps; I only had a gut feeling that serving there wasn't 'right,' as well as a more reasoned, philosophical judgment that this violated the ethical code of a doctor. Years later, after being imprisoned by the Americans, I learned the true nature of the crimes carried out in the concentration camps and was relieved I had rejected all offers made.

Those imprisoned in the three camps I visited were political prisoners, Jews, homosexuals, Jehovah's Witnesses, Catholic priests, communists, and everyone else who did not fit into Nazi ideology. Unlike those in Poland and Czechoslovakia, these three camps did not have gas chambers. Despite this, many detainees in the camps I visited died due to horrific working and living conditions, hunger, typhoid, other diseases, medical experiments and plain cruelty.

SS MEDICAL ACADEMY, 3RD TO 6TH SEMESTER

As a member of the SS Medical Academy, I pursued my medical studies at the University of Graz from April 1942 until June 1944. Finally, I could study for two consecutive years, despite the constant threat of being summoned back to the front. In June 1942, the SS promoted me to the rank of Untersturmführer, which is comparable to Second Lieutenant. As I rose in rank, I received higher military pay. From February 1943 through January 1944, I served as adjutant at the SS Medical Academy, where I assisted the commanding officer with personnel decisions and Academy administration.

> 'The POW [Sepp Salmutter] received a poor efficiency rating. He was constantly criticized for his weakness of character, lack of friendliness, and total lack of personal traits, which typified the SS man. He was criticized for choosing to spend insufficient time at the officers' mess, preferring to be with his old friends in Graz, friends who were under suspicion by the SS. The POW claims that this attitude didn't worry him because he hoped that this alone would mean an early discharge [from the SS] once the war was over.' [Curriculum vitae]

That's what it says in my US Intelligence file. I hoped to continue my life as a civilian doctor, rather than serve as a medic in the army.

At university, I took the following courses: Physiology, Skin and Venereal Diseases, Dentistry, Ophthalmology, ENT, Obstetrics and Pediatrics, Pharmacology and practical training in trauma surgery, the field in which I would specialize later in life.

Students from the Wehrmacht who enrolled in courses that assisted the war effort could obtain leave from front line duty in order to study for a few semesters or, if lucky, for the entire duration of their degree course. Groups of young men formed, who would study together and, upon graduating, go off to war together.

I wore my black SS uniform to lectures, which aroused suspicion in some and respect in others. In co-ed classes and the lab, I got to know some female students who invited me to film screenings and events organized by the German student union. My uniform attracted some hot Nazi girls, and they naturally latched on to me. They would escort me through the city and, with luck, accompany me back to my academy digs.

To avoid the bombing raids, the people of Graz blacked out their homes at night, but it was still safe to walk around. The so-called 'Folk Community' stuck together, and there were few break-ins, robberies, or street assaults.

I wasn't interested in going to the theatre, except for Nestroy vaudeville plays, which always made me laugh. I had read enough classics like Goethe and Shakespeare during my schooldays, while all Jewish authors' plays were frowned upon and their performances canceled.

In dry weather, as in high school, a small group of us would hike into the nearby mountains, where I found peace and comfort among nature, far away from human habitation.

Ausſchuß für die ärztliche Vorprüfung

nach Erlaß des Herrn Reichs-
innenministers vom 31. 1. 1941,
IV-d 3784/41/3590-

in Graz

Nr. 306 W. Nr.

Überſicht 8. XII. 43
5. I. 44

Prüfungsbeginn:

über die ärztliche Vorprüfung be Studierenden S a l m u t t e r Sepp

geboren am 31. Jänner 1921 in Semriach, Steierm.

wohnhaft in Graz. Rosenberggürtel Nr.12. Staatsange-

Prüfungsfach	Name des Prüfers	Tag, Monat und Jahr der Prüfung	Einzelurteil (in Worten)	Eigenhändige Unterſch des Prüfers	teil jedes in
1	2	3	4	5	6
I. Anatomie	Prof.Dr.Anton Hafferl	7/8 43	gut	*[signature]*	
	Prof.Dr.Alfred Pischinger	7/8.43	sehr gut	Pischinger	
Wiederholung					2 x5=
IIa. Allgemeine Phyſiologie	Prof.Dr.Leop. Löhner	8.10.1943	nicht er-schienen	Löhner	
Wiederholung		28.I.1944	genügend	Löhner	
					Summe II a+II
IIb. Phyſiologiſche Chemie	Prof.Dr.Hans Lieb	8.10.1943	nicht angetreten	Lieb	
Wiederholung		26.1.1944	gut	Lieb	abgerundet 1 x5=
III. Phyſik	Prof.Dr.Erich Rumpf				3 x2=
Wiederholung					
IV. Chemie	Prof.Dr.Hans Lieb	27.7.1942	genügend	H. Lieb	3
Wiederholung					
Va. Zoologie	Prof.Dr.Josef Meixner	27.7.42	gut	Meixner	
Wiederholung					Summe Va + V
Vb. Botanik	Prof.Dr.Rud. Scharfetter	24.7.42	sehr gut	Scharfetter	
Wiederholung					abgerundet 2 x1=
					Summe 39

Die Prüfung ist bestanden am 28. Jänner 1944 mit dem Gesamturteil: genügend

Graz, den 28. Jänner 1944

Der Vorsitzende Pischinger

Der letzte Prüfungstag ist in der Übersicht zu unterstreichen.

Examinations passed by Salmutter at Graz University, 1941-1944

Nightly philosophical discussions about God, the world, providence, or Darwin left me cold. I was indifferent to such topics and preferred to study or meet female friends from the provinces, looking for some adventures away from their parental control. 'Live now, for tomorrow you might die' was the motto for young people in those uncertain times.

Sometimes I accompanied comrades to the railway station on their journey to the front. To hide our fear, we joked and laughed until the train left for the Eastern front. We told ourselves we would all meet again after the Final Victory, but once the last wagon had disappeared into the night fog, I would go home depressed, thinking of the bloody battles ahead for my comrades.

Whenever the weather permitted, I studied in the nearby city park. At least, I tried. Distractions came not only from young girls passing by, but also from tame squirrels and titmice scrounging for scraps. These made me forget my worries – and sometimes my studies. I preferred sitting alone in the park to joining my noisy comrades in the officers' mess.

Until the summer of 1944, the food situation wasn't so bad. The SS Medical Academy catered for all our needs, and we received ration cards we could use in the local restaurants. The female students and the young men in uniform, whether Wehrmacht or SS, were pleased to stay at university throughout the war. Though the daily restrictions affected our lives, we could still work toward our professional careers in relative safety. However, in the back of my mind, there remained a gut feeling that one day I would return to serve at the front.

GRETL GLATZ

Herwig, at this point, I would like to explain a bit more about your mother and her relatives. Gretl Glatz was born in Graz on July 1, 1921

In the Moral Questionnaire at Fort Hunt, I described Gretl's father, Dr. Hans Glatz, as a Nazi opponent:

> 'Senior Medical Officer Dr. Hans Glatz, hospital director in St. Pölten near Vienna, member of the Masonic Lodge, non-denominational and positive resistance to the Nazis. After the Anschluss of Austria, he could only regain his position as hospital director once a certain period of his dismissal had passed and after a student friend of his had become Gauleiter [provincial leader] (Dr. Jury*).' [questionnaire].
>
> * In March 1938, Dr. Jury joined the SS with the rank of Sturmbannführer. In April 1938, he was elected a Nazi member of the Reichstag. In May 1938, Hitler appointed him to be the Nazi Party Gauleiter of the Reichsgau Niederdonau. Hugo Jury was an ardent advocate of Nazi racial policies. He supported the persecution of Jews, Sinti, and Roma and the mentally or physically incapacitated. Toward the end of the war, Jury, a fanatical Nazi, continued to call for armed resistance, personally commanding a Volkssturm force against Soviet forces. After the final collapse of Nazi Germany, on the night of May 8, 1945, Hugo Jury committed suicide by shooting himself. He was reputed to have been one of the lovers of the soprano Elisabeth Schwarzkopf.

Gretl's father did not want me to marry his daughter. First and foremost, I did not belong to a middle-class family, and second, I was a member of the SS. He had little regard for the Nazis or the SS; in his eyes they were unwashed rabble-rousers. Despite this, he became a Nazi collaborator and joined the NSDAP in order to keep his job.

Der Führer

hat mit Erlaß vom heutigen Tage

den Direktor d.Krankenhauses und Prosektor

Dr.Hans G l a t z

St.Pölten

als Anerkennung für 25 jährige treue Dienste

das

filberne

Treudienft=Ehrenzeichen

verliehen.

Berlin, den

Der Staatsminifter
und Chef der Präfidialkanzlei
des Führers und Reichskanzlers

Gretl's father, Dr Hans Glatz, joined the National Socialist Party after the Anschluss of Austria in order to be able to remain in his post as hospital director

Diploma for 25 years service as hospital director

Gerti, the second wife of Dr. Hans Glatz, Gretl's stepmother

**Gretl's mother, Maria Bychkova, medical student,
St. Petersburg, Russia, 1912**

Hans Glatz had gone to grammar school in Pettau, Lower Styria, today part of Slovenia. He finished his obligatory one-year military service with the Austrian Imperial and Royal Army in Riva on Lake Garda a few years before the First World War, then, as the son of wealthy parents, he'd studied medicine in Vienna and Berlin. After joining the army as a volunteer at the start of the war, his laid-back lifestyle took a drastic turn. The Russians defeated the Austrian army in Galicia, and he was taken prisoner-of-war.

The 1917 Russian revolution delayed his return home by several years. He turned down an opportunity to go home early, enabling his critically ill friend Lauda to go instead. He became embroiled in battles between the revolutionary Red Guards and the White Guards who were loyal followers of the Tsar and the former government. When the Bolshevik Reds took over the latter's hospital train, they slaughtered the entire crew, including the doctors, and renamed it after the dead German communist, Karl Liebknecht. Hans Glatz became a member of the medical staff. He kept a diary about his wartime experiences, but it was confiscated by a suspicious Soviet commissar before he returned to Austria.

On the hospital train, Hans fell in love with a colleague, Doctor Maria Bytschkowa, and they married. Maria was the daughter of a wealthy Russian merchant who had settled in Tashkent in Central Asia. Maria had studied medicine in St. Petersburg and was a young divorcee when she met my father-in-law.

After seven years in captivity, in 1920 Hans Glatz returned to Leoben with his new Russian bride. His mother welcomed him home by saying, 'That woman needs to go back home right away!' My father-in-law refused to send her back, and a year later, his Russian wife bore him a daughter, Gretl, who would later become my wife.

Hans Glatz, now over the age of thirty, finished his medical studies in Graz. Given the post-war years and the responsibilities of providing for a young family, he could no longer pursue a time-consuming and low-paying research career. Instead, he took over as director of the hospital in St. Pölten, though the post of a university professor would have been his preferred choice.

Gretl's paternal ancestors originated from Gottschee, a German-speaking enclave in what is now Slovenia. Gretl's grandpa traveled as a merchant in neighboring countries before settling in Leoben, in the Austrian province of Styria. He grew his modest business into a vast enterprise, supplying the entire Enns, Mürz and upper Mur valleys, as well as operating a cheese trade delivering as far away as Hungary. In addition, he bought several residential houses in the town center. He was a tough character: when elderly and ailing, and needing to be pushed around in a wheelchair, he would brandish his walking stick to scare away passers-by who got in his way.

He divorced his wife, drawing condemnation from the Catholic Church, and thus he renounced his beliefs. Meanwhile, his ex-wife – Gretl's grandmother – was equally obstinate. She ignored their divorce and continued to work in the business as before; when her ex-husband suggested remarrying after a few years, she declined.

Gretl's grandparents conceived three sons. The eldest was Gretl's father, Hans, whom they called Jonny. Andreas and Karl were the other two. Andreas studied law in Vienna. His first son fell at Stalingrad in 1942, and his younger son, Heinz, followed in his father's footsteps, becoming a lawyer in Vienna. Karl inherited the majority of the properties in Leoben along with the delicatessen business. Sadly, he was not as successful as his father and leased the business out to the fish restaurant chain, 'Nordsee'. The imposing family headstone in the Leoben cemetery attests to the Glatz family's prominence at its peak.

Despite being a doctor in Russia, Gretl's mother Maria (1891-1929) had to re-enroll in Austria for several semesters, before earning a further doctorate from the University of Graz. She opened a dentistry practice, but soon afterwards succumbed to an infectious disease and died; Gretl was eight years old at the time.

Hans Glatz, widowed for two years, married his beautiful second wife, Gertrude, nicknamed Gerti, with whom he was endlessly infatuated. She was twenty-four, and he was forty-three; she was from Olmütz in Moravia and had moved to St. Pölten with her parents when the Austro-Hungarian empire collapsed.

Gerti and Hans both made a 'good catch.' She was sociable, outgoing and charismatic, and took over the family finances once they had married. She had Hans wrapped around her little finger, whilst being free to do whatever she pleased. Gerti was only thirteen years older than her eleven-year-old stepdaughter when she married Hans.

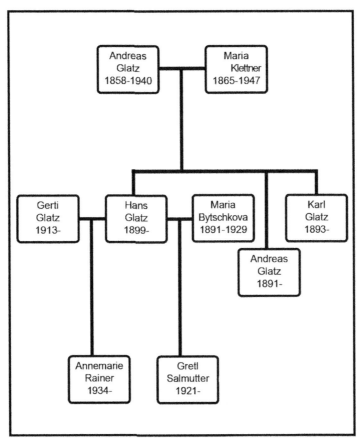

Family tree of Gretl Salmutter, neé Glatz

She was wholly unprepared for the role of parenthood, so it should come as no surprise Gerti and Gretl did not get along from the start. Gretl's half-sister, Annemarie, was born in 1934, one year after her parents married. Until early 1945, the family resided in St. Pölten, in the director's flat at the regional hospital.

With her husband's reluctant approval, Gerti enrolled Gretl at the Catholic Ursulines boarding school in Graz. After school, she went to study medicine at the University of Graz, continuing to visit her family in St. Pölten. But Gretl and her stepmother grew further and further apart, and she was pushed out of the family, though her father still supported her financially throughout her studies.

MARRIAGE

In the 'Moral Questionnaire' I had to complete while interned at Fort Hunt, I stated the following about my marriage:

> 'In June 1942 the POW Salmutter and Miss Margarete Glatz, medical student, daughter of Obermedizinalrat Dr. Hans Glatz of St. Pölten, decided to marry. Since Miss Glatz's mother, Maria, neé Bytschkowa, was born to Russian parents in Tashkent, Turkestan, she could not supply the required proof of pure Aryan ancestry. The POW was constantly reproached for this by his superiors and his "SS Kameraden," who considered his behavior most unlike that of an SS man.' [questionnaire]

> 'The "SS Rasse- and Siedlungshauptamt" (The SS Race and Settlement Office) in Berlin wanted to conduct an anthropological examination of his fiancée, but the POW insisted he would marry her and asked to be released from the SS.' [questionnaire]

> 'In the meantime, the commander of the Medical Academy in Graz intervened. He granted him permission to marry without this certificate of pure Aryan ancestry on the condition that as soon as the war was over, this certificate had to be filed. If this could not be done, marriage would be declared illegal.' [questionnaire]

> 'The couple married in Vienna on February 27, 1943.' [Curriculum vitae]

I made this partially false statement to the Americans, intending to depict myself as an unwilling Nazi follower, who had pursued a love match in defiance of the Race Laws. The US authorities couldn't prove or disprove my claim; from my point of view, I had no choice but to try

Sehr geehrter Herr.Dr. G l a t z !

Erst am 31.Dezember 1942 ist auf vielen Umwegen Ihr
Schreiben vom 21.12. in meine Hände gelangt. Man hat
mir seinerzeit, unmittelbar im Anschluß an den Brief
Ihrer Frau Gemahlin an mich, gemeldet, daß Ihr Fräulein
Tochter keinerlei Wert mehr darauf legt den SS-Untersturmführer S a l m u t t e r zu heiraten. Ich hatte
S a l m u t t e r den strikten Befehl zur größtmöglichen
Beschleunigung der Eheangelegenheit gegeben. Angeblich
bestehen jedoch seitens Ihres Fräulein Tochters Bindungen
zu einem anderen Manne, der auch, wie mir gesagt wurde,
die Tatsache, daß Ihr Fräulein Tochter ein Kind von
S a l m u t t e r erwartet, ohne weiteres mit in Kauf
zu nehmen gewillt ist.

Unter diesen Umständen halte ich es für richtig, sehr geehrter Herr Doktor, daß Sie sich vielleicht zunächst ein-
mal mit Ihrem Fräulein Tochter unmittelbar ins Benehmen
setzen und feststellen, ob die von mir eben geschilderten
Verhältnisse den Tatsachen entsprechen. Ich persönlich
hatte und habe keinerlei keinerlei Veranlassung an der
Wahrheit der mir gemachten Meldung zu zweifeln.

Sollten sich irgendwelche Unstimmigkeiten ergeben, so wäre
ich für eine Benachrichtigung Ihrerseits dankbar, damit
ich dann den erforderlichen Druck auf S a l m u t t e r
ausüben kann.

Mit dem Ausdruck der vorzüglichsten Hochachtung und

Heil Hitler!

SS-Obersturmbannführer

**Letter from Salmutter's superior, Commander
of the Medical Academy, Dr. med. H Kaether,
SS Obersturmbannführer, to Salmutter's future
father-in-law, Dr. Hans Glatz, with the promise to
'excert the necessary pressure on Sepp Salmutter'
to enter into marriage with his daughter**

Graz, 4 January 1943

Dear Dr. G l a t z !

It was not until 31 December 1942 that your letter of 21 December after many detours reached my hands. Immediately after receiving your wife's letter, I was informed that your daughter no longer attaches any importance to marrying SS-Untersturmführer Salmutter.

I had given Salmutter strict orders to expedite the marriage as quickly as possible. Allegedly, however, your daughter appears to have ties to another man who, as I was told, is willing to accept the fact that your daughter is expecting a child by Salmutter.

Under these circumstances, Dear Doctor, I think it would be right for you to first of all contact your daughter directly and find out whether the circumstances I have just described correspond to the facts. Personally, I had and have no reason to doubt the truth of the report made to me.

If any discrepancies arise, I would be grateful for a notification from you so that I can then put the necessary pressure on Salmutter.

With the expression of the highest esteem and

Heil Hitler!

Dozent Dr. med. H. Kaether
SS-Obersturmbannführer

KAETHER, Hans: (46) SS Obersturmbannführer and physician. C.O. of the SS Medical Academy in GRAZ until the summer of 1943. Party member; resides in PRAG (?). High government and party connections which he uses to his own advantage. By using his political influence he was successful in placing himself on the staff of the University of Graz for the sole purpose of checking politically on the professors. Took part in many important conferences at the academy. good connections with the Gestapo. Last seen during the summer of 1943 in GRAZ. Middle-sized, heavy set. Heavy drinker*.

* one of the 52 mini-biographies which Sepp Salmutter prepared for US Intelligence in 1945

to save my skin. The Nuremberg trial preparations were in full swing, which resulted in me being labeled a member of a criminal organization. So, in the questionnaire, I stated that I would have quit the SS if I had been forced to abandon my bride. For the rewards offered to me by the SS, I sacrificed everything. I did not reveal that you were born only seven days after our wedding, helping to make the story of a loving marriage all the more convincing. Had the Americans discovered this, our late wedding ceremony could have been blamed on slow-working Nazi bureaucracy.

Now, let me tell you the truth. After returning from the Military Academy in Braunschweig in April 1942, I continued my medical studies in Graz, where I lived at the SS Medical Academy. Gretl was one of several young ladies I courted. She was from a middle-class family and had led quite a sheltered life. I ran into her four weeks after my return to Graz. The Academy permitted us to bring back a female companion once a week to stay overnight. I regularly invited a variety of young women. Therefore, three months later, after having almost forgotten Gretl, I was stunned when she came to tell me she was pregnant with my child. And so it all began!

Under these new circumstances, Gretl's father could no longer object to my marrying into the Glatz family. But I did not want to be tied down. Gretl had received a proposal from an older man, who would have accepted you as his own child, but Gretl and I eventually gave in to social and familial pressure and got married.

Marriage in Vienna on 27 February 1943 :
Hans Glatz, Karl Glatz, Gretl and Sepp Salmutter

My superior at the Medical Academy had compelled me to marry Gretl, saying, 'You can't desert a young woman with a child!' Gretl was unable to show 100% Aryan descent, and under the Nuremberg Race Laws the marriage would be legal only until the end of the war. I secretly hoped that at some point I could back out of my commitment. I kept all of this hidden from the Yanks while imprisoned at Fort Hunt, pretending instead to have fought the SS racists and to have exchanged vows with a woman who was, due to her ancestry in Tashkent, in all possibility non-Aryan.

In Vienna, on February 27, 1943, I married Fräulein Gretl Glatz. Her father and her uncle Karl attended the wedding, but Gerti stayed at home. She thought I was unworthy to be her stepson. I presented myself in full SS regalia, with a ceremonial dagger at my hip. Gretl's uncle Karl, who often bragged about being an enthusiastic Nazi, fawned over my uniform, Gretl hid her advanced pregnancy beneath a heavy coat, and we all tried our hardest to put on a happy front.

After you were born, Herwig, you and Gretl moved into her student flat, while I stayed at the SS Medical Academy. We would get together a few times a week. It took a long time for me to forgive Gretl for the marriage I felt had been imposed upon me. After you were born, she continued to study attending lectures whenever she could. Our wedding had been solely motivated by your impending birth.

FRENCH CAMPAIGN, 1944

I finished my sixth semester at the University of Graz in June 1944, when you were fifteen months old. In the end, the call I'd been dreading arrived. The next time I saw you, you would be four. At the front, I served as an Untersturmführer and assistant doctor in the 2nd Medical Company of the 2nd SS Panzer Division, Das Reich's central dressing station. I would have much preferred to stay in Graz and further my education.

The Panzer, Panzer Grenadier, Infantry, Artillery Regiment, anti-aircraft gunners, Assault Gunners, Rocket Launchers, Reconnaissance and Intelligence Divisions and supply units comprised the 2nd SS Panzer Division. The Divisional Doctor commanded the medical companies assigned to each Division.

Throughout the two years I'd spent in medical studies at the Graz Academy from 1942 to 1944, my Panzer Division, Das Reich, had waged a devastating war on the Eastern Front. In February 1944, the Headquarters of the Wehrmacht relocated the Division back to the Toulouse area in southwestern France for 'refreshing,' which in army jargon meant replacing fallen soldiers with new ones. Seventy railway trains were necessary to transport the entire Division.

Previous military operations and violent encounters had influenced the officers and non-commissioned officers. Those radicalized National Socialists planned to commit the same atrocities against the French as they had against the Soviets in the east. The SS Panzer Division Das Reich left a trail of carnage everywhere it fought. The Division Commander had ordered acts of severe reprisal against partisans, and I witnessed multiple incidents that violated the Geneva War Convention.

'We medics, as part of our Division, had just slipped out of an encircled area when an American rocket bomber arrived and bombed the armored car positioned there on the road, and there was one of our medics who heard the rockets coming down but didn't know exactly what they were aiming at; he couldn't see it, and he ran behind the armored car for cover... and that's how he ran straight into the path of the rocket bombardment.

We ran away from the armored car and were spared because they didn't attack us, not our medics, but only the columns of tanks... A few minutes later, after the bomber had passed, when we returned to the spot, we saw that one from our medical group was dead.

That's when our Obersturmführer got very angry. We had a few wounded Americans in our custody. And this Obersturmführer wanted immediate reprisals against the Americans. If you want to be objective, the Americans bombed this place, and our medic ran into the line of fire and got hit. All of us who stayed with our vehicles were unhurt. We had driven off the road into the open field...

The Obersturmführer immediately pulled two Americans, an officer and one other, down from our ambulance, where they were sitting on straw, and led them to the place where our medic had been hit. The corpse still sported the Red Cross armband. The Obersturmführer told the Yanks, "Look here, a Red Cross man! Your comrades killed him." He was about ready to kill the two Americans when, fortunately, the Hauptsturmführer came along and gave the Obersturmführer a good mouthful.' [eavesdropped]

SS Untersturmführer Sepp Salmutter, 1944

Following the Allied invasion of Normandy on June 6, 1944, our Division received the command to fight them back to the beaches. In response to the increasing French resistance, our Division on its journey north from Toulouse committed heinous war crimes against citizens accused of collaborating with the Résistance. In Tulle, the Waffen SS hanged 99 citizens who had been charged with assisting the Résistance, from lamp-posts and balconies as punishment for the killing of 40 German soldiers. In Oradour-sur-Glane, the Waffen SS locked 642 residents inside a church before setting fire to it, burning everyone alive. I did not support inhuman warfare or the murder of civilians, and one of the brutal SS commanders reprimanded me:

> *'I was known as a soft Austrian because fanaticism never suited me. My commander gave me a severe reprimand because I gave medical help to wounded Belgian civilians; that was purely human! What a bunch of barbarians.' [eavesdropped]*

My technique of not hearing, seeing, or saying anything began to fall apart. I began to see, hear, and think but could not say anything, because doing so would have amounted to a death sentence immediate transfer to a suicide mission on the Eastern Front. How long would I be able to keep this pact with the devil, now I saw it for what it was? I could see catastrophe approaching, but did it mean I'd be able to avoid it? Could I ever atone for my sins?

My Division came under attack once again during the Battle of Normandy, and on our retreat from France and Belgium. Due to substantial German defeats and losses of both troops and resources, the Division had to be with-drawn in October 1944 and 'refreshed' near the former Reich's boundary, not far from Cologne, at the Siegfried Line we called the West Wall.

In terms of troops, weaponry, and equipment, the Waffen SS competed with the Wehrmacht from the start. Because the German armaments industry was unable to meet the needs of frontline troops, the SS received the best equip-ment due to its superior reliability and fighting morale. The heavy Waffen SS tank Divisions, which operated independently within the Panzer Divisions, used the most impressive tank units – the famed Tiger and Königstiger tanks. The flagship units – Leibstandarte-SS Adolf Hitler, my Division Das Reich, and Totenkopf – were prioritized in resource allocation and upgraded to elite units. The SS deployed their Divisions to dangerous areas and, in some cases, they suffered heavy losses. New supplies had to be found to re-equip the SS units, sometimes using stocks captured from the Allies. In the Ardennes, for example, I drove over the battlefields in a US jeep, picking up wounded soldiers and transporting them to a nearby field hospital.

You'd probably like to know, Herwig, when I started toying with the idea of desertion. When did I first become aware of the injustice and futility of this war? Or was it something else I'd realized: that I might not be on the winning side and I needed to find a way out before it was too late. As you will soon see, it all happened far faster than I had anticipated.

My doubts began to surface near the end of 1944. We sustained significant losses at the beginning of September 1944 after fierce battles with the Americans, who had entered the war in June and who forced us to retreat back toward the German border. Many of my comrades had fallen, and we were out of heavy weaponry, all the while American planes continued to attack us mercilessly.

Though we had painted white crosses on our jeeps and were easily identified as medics on the battlefield, grenades detonated all around us. I hurled myself to the ground during one such incident, when a shrapnel hit my right leg, near my buttock. After my five-inch flesh wound had been disinfected, stitched and bandaged, I had to operate and care for the wounded in the tent hospital for a fortnight instead of serving on the battlefield. My wound healed without any complications.

Our units could not move because of chronic fuel shortages, and the Allies' air superiority grew. We quickly reassembled units by reinforcing the Siegfried Line and the Reich's western boundary north and south of Aachen. By late October 1944, we had been pushed back into old Reich territory on all fronts.

Aachen was the first German city to surrender to the Allies in October 1944. The Wehrmacht found itself in a difficult predicament, fighting East and West on two fronts. The Allies were vastly superior to us and expected to maintain the initiative. I began to doubt whether we could win this war.

FURLOUGH IN GRAZ

In November 1944, whilst stationed at the Siegfried Line and following the destruction of Graz by Allied bombing raids, my commander permitted me to go home on furlough to find alternative accommodation for my family and ensure their safety.

The train from Cologne to Graz was on schedule. On the journey, I got food rations, and sleeping on the train wasn't too uncomfortable. I was 23 years old and travelling in uniform. 'Be thankful you're still alive,' I reminded myself. I carried my soldier's ID with me, as it was a requirement under the law for soldiers to produce an identity card. It specified the purpose and date of my trip: a ten-day leave of absence from Cologne to Graz and return, with the reason stated 'recreational leave.' On the bottom it bore my army commander's signature.

When I returned to Graz, I was shocked to see observing the massive devastation of my hometown in the area around the railway station and to the north of the city. These strikes highlighted both the Allies' power and weakness of the German defenses.

> *'Bomb damage is the result of the attack of November 1, 1944. The prisoner saw this during furlough in his hometown.'*
> *[office correspondence]*

After the American invasion of Normandy in June 1944, the prospect of defeat became more realistic. In Graz,

I enjoyed a brief reprieve from the horrors of war but what would happen to me next? I hadn't yet devised a viable plan allowing me to elude the Waffen SS and survive the war unscathed. All I wanted at the time was to enjoy these few days at home, away from the brutal violence.

I couldn't find you or your mother in Graz. Gretl had been bombed out and had fled west to avoid falling into the clutches of the Russians, whose unstoppable advance was drawing ever closer.

I reported to the SS Medical Academy to arrange my lodging for a few nights. There I met Carl Edmund Schlink, the SS Oberführer and doctor. He asked if I could come to his house for dinner in a couple of days. He wanted to invite a few friends and to hear about my most recent war adventures. I agreed.

The next day, I went to Niederschöckl, a two-hour hike from Maria-Trost to the Sternwirt Inn on top of a hill, then back down to the settlement. The atmosphere was gloomy and solemn. While our able-bodied soldiers fought on the front, detained farm laborers from Eastern European territories supported the farmers. An underage Polish maid worked for my grandmother and uncle. Uncle told me that Alois, the farmhand, had been drafted in 1940 and fallen in the winter of 1942 near Stalingrad. This news depressed me. Uncle had been ruled ineligible to enlist due to his thick glasses.

My grandmother, who was in her seventies now, fed the chickens. For her, fieldwork had become too laborious.

SALMUTTER, Sepp
SS Obersturmfuehrer
I./SS Pz Art Regt "Das Reich"
21 Jan '45, GOUVY, Belgium

SECRET

6 June 1945.

Capt. Brown

     P/W is a young and intelligent Austrian medical officer who deserted to the American forces. He is most cooperative and friendly. Believed to be very reliable. P/W worked for FID in NAMUR from the latter part of January to 5 April 1945.

...itional Report on PERSONALITIES:

(Numbers in parentheses indicate approximate ages.)

SCHLINK, Carl-Edmund: (40) SS Oberfuehrer and physician. C.O. of the SS Medical Academy in GRAZ from April '44 until the present. Resides at Rosenbergguertel 12 in GRAZ. Party member and fanatical Nazi, but as a human being righteous and honorable. Was always having difficulty with his superior, Brigadefuehrer, Dr. Genzken, of the SS Sanitaets Hauptamt. During the occupation of France, in Toulouse as Div. Surgeon for SS Div "Das Reich." An extremely heavy drinker. Tall, dark blonde, excellent military posture, sabre wounds in face. Last seen November 1944 in GRAZ.

POESCHL, Walter: (35) SS Hauptsturmfuehrer and physician. Director of a course at the SS Medical Academy in GRAZ. Party member prior to the Anschluss. Resides in GRAZ, Zinzendorfgasse. Medium-size, dark, red face, Native Austrian, not active politically. November 1944 still in GRAZ.

JOKUSCH, Walter: (37) SS Sturmbannfuehrer and physician. Director of a course at the SS Medical School in GRAZ. Resides in GRAZ in Rosenbergguertel. Party member; 100% Nazi, but known to be extremely stupid. Tall, blonde, blue eyes, heavy-set. Eats and drinks excessively. In November 1944 still in GRAZ.

ERRLINGER, Helmut: (27) SS Obersturmfuehrer and former student at the SS Medical Academy in GRAZ. Received Iron Cross I class while medical officer with Leibstandarte "Adolf Hitler" in Normandy. Party member; resides in Jungfrauengasse in GRAZ. Tall, dark blonde, thin. Speaks Swabian dialect. Stool pigeon for the officers in charge of the academy; watched over and secretly judged fellow students. Father is a high SS officer. Last seen in November 1944 in GRAZ.

SCHIELE, Horst: (27) SS Obersturmfuehrer and medical student at the SS Medical Academy in GRAZ. Party member. Married; resides in Humboldtstr in GRAZ. Very tall, dark blonde; stupid and Prussian. 100% Nazi. Last seen in GRAZ in November 1944.

BAUMECKER, Martin: (29) SS Obersturmfuehrer and physician. Student at the SS Medical Academy in GRAZ. Party member; residence unknown. Tall, dark, soft voice. Lukewarm Nazi; kept postponing taking doctors' exam so he would not be sent to the front. Shipped to front in November 1944.

SS officers present at the SS Medical Academy in Graz in November 1944

I feared she was still resentful of my membership in the Waffen SS. There was enough wood to heat the stove in the kitchen/dining/living room, keeping it comfortably warm and cozy. The pork she prepared had been preserved in fat and stored in the barn to keep it well hidden from the Nazi administrators.

Despite the war, the villagers were preparing for Christmas. Reports from the front were of no interest anymore. They had heard enough about the defeats and retreats and, worst of all, the fallen acquaintances, friends, and family members. What a stark contrast to earlier years, back in 1940, when the villagers had been eager to hear about my victories at the front and to learn what France was like with all those legendarily lusty French women!

The village of Niederschöckl had made little progress, with its squat dwellings, small windows and no running water or electricity. The villagers had always endured a rough existence, mostly devoid of comforts. They spent their days toiling in the fields, feeding their families, raising children, and going to church. Life went on as usual, and as was the case all over the country, Nazi fanatics lived cheek-by-jowl with others who were sick of war.

As I walked back to Graz, it was getting dark, snow was falling, and it was getting chilly. I couldn't get Alois out of my mind as I recalled joyful childhood memories.

The day of my invitation to Schlink's house arrived. I want to recount this event to provide some insight into the officers' attitudes on the home front at the end of 1944.

I arrived at the four-story, mid-nineteenth-century house on Rosenberggürtel. Graz University was only a few minutes away. A magnificent and spectacular staircase with wide stairs fashioned in marble and stone brought me up to his second-floor apartment. Such cool stone staircases would provide a pleasant reprieve from the outdoor heat in summer; but in winter they were icy.

Schlink's elegant middle-aged wife opened the door. 'Good day, Herr Untersturmführer. Other gentlemen are waiting for you in the living room.'

Two more guests arrived after me, bringing the total to seven. All were either doctors or medical students. Some, such as SS Oberführer Schlink, wore civilian clothes. Others like me arrived in full uniform. Once we arrived in the living room, the host handed us cigarettes and pear schnapps to warm us all up and break the ice. 'I'm not permitted to smoke cigars because my wife can't handle the stink,' Schlink explained.

After some time, the maid opened the dining room divider and led us to the table. She asked Schlink whether she could begin serving right away. 'Sure,' Schlink replied, turning to face the guests, 'and it was my wife who cooked the dinner.'

The young maid, wearing a white pinafore on top of a short dark dress and black cotton stockings, served the frittata soup, followed by roast pork, sauerkraut and potatoes, complemented by local Gösser beer or wine. The maid served each guest a salad of sliced cucumber in vinegar and Styrian pumpkin seed oil. She later served us warm apple strudel with vanilla sauce for dessert. Finally, Schlink passed around cognac and more cigarettes to cap off this bizarre gentlemen's evening.

Carl Edmund Schlink, our host, was around forty years old, tall, with dark blond hair and various scars on his face. He was an SS Oberführer, as well as a medical doctor. SS Oberführer is a high military-grade officer position between SS Standartenführer and SS Brigadeführer, and the uniforms had embroidered foliage on the collars and braided shoulder pieces. He became a top officer of the SS Medical Academy in Graz in April 1944 and was a party member and passionate National Socialist, but still a decent and honorable person. His relationship with his superior, Brigadeführer Doktor Genzkon of the SS Medical Main Administration, was always complex. I first encountered Schlink during the German occupation of France in 1940, when he'd been a Divisional doctor in the 2nd SS Panzer Division Das Reich. I also knew him to be a chronic alcoholic.

Two more comrades I knew by name sat at the table with me. One of them was Horst Schiele, a twenty-seven-year-old SS Obersturmführer and SS Academy medical student. He was married and lived in Graz's Humboldtstrasse. Tall, dark blond, Prussian and stupid, he was a member of the Party and a zealous Nazi.

Martin Baumecker was the other one. He was 29 years old, and SS Obersturmführer, a student at the SS Medical Academy in Graz, and a member of the Party. He was dark haired and soft spoken; a lukewarm Nazi who had postponed his doctor's examination in order to avoid serving at the front.

We maintained our small talk at the dinner table. Martin was chatting about a torchlight parade toward Adolf Hitler Square, the former Main Square, when Schlink interrupted him with a loud burp whilst holding his wine glass in his left hand. After an uneasy pause, hitting his chest hard with his open right hand, Schlink declared, 'I now declare this bazaar open.'

I'm not sure if we roared out of embarrassment or sheer delight. Schlink had created an atmosphere like the officers' mess. All that remained was for someone to fart and accuse the fictitious dog, and everything would be back to normal. I had never enjoyed this kind of companionship before and had always avoided the officers' mess like the plague. But I played along, pretending to be at ease and in good company.

Schlink requested that as guest of honor I report from the front. I explained why I was here, claiming I had come to look for new lodgings for my wife and son, who had been made homeless due to intense allied bombing. I couldn't help them because they had fled to the western part of the country to avoid the Russians invading from the east.

'The English and Americans are only attacking our train station, not residential neighborhoods here in the eastern city center; we should be safe, so drink up!' Schlink added, raising his glass.

Helmut Ehrlinger, twenty-seven-year-old, SS Obersturm-führer, Party member and former student at the SS Medical Academy in Graz, was the evening's next speaker.

While serving as an officer in the 1st SS Panzer Division Leibstandarte Adolf Hitler in Normandy, he'd received the Iron Cross, First Class. He deserved our admiration! He resided in Graz's Jungfrauengasse, was tall and lanky and spoke in a south German dialect. We suspected him of spying on us and drafting secret reports on fellow Academy officials and pupils. His father was a high-ranking SS officer. 'Wait until we have our weapons of vengeance, and we'll throw the Americans back into the sea,' he threatened.

I ended up discussing my wound. 'In September, I was hit in the ass by a shell, a cannon shot. The projectile exploded right above me, but I was lucky; the poor guy next to me didn't survive the attack.'

'Sepp, are your balls still hanging...?' inquired Horst.

'Yes, yes, both are still in working order,' I replied, to loud laughter.

Following that, I spoke of an incident at the front where an American bombardment had killed one of our medics. 'In retaliation, our Obersturmführer planned to put two kidnapped Americans against the wall. He would have shot them had the Hauptsturmführer not intervened.'

'Well, I would have killed those Yanks,' said Walter Jokusch, interrupting the conversation. Walter enjoyed boasting, but he did all he could to avoid serving at the front. He held a high position as an SS Sturmbannführer, was a doctor who taught at the SS Medical Academy, and lived nearby on Rosenberggürtel. He was a Party member and another zealous Nazi – sturdily built and well-known for his stupidity. If he were an animal, I'd compare him to a blue-eyed gorilla. Despite being taught better manners at the SS Junker School, he ate and drank excessively and spoke with his mouth full.

'Oh no, Herr Sturmbannführer,' Schlink exclaimed as he turned to face Jokusch. 'After all, we're not Bolsheviks, and executing captured Americans is against a soldier's honor. The important thing is we keep them out of action.'

I remained noncommittal throughout the chat. Was this the last dance on the volcano before the regime erupted? I tried not to criticize the war effort. You never knew how things might be interpreted and who felt what... Fortunately, thoughts were still free. 'Our Air Force won't protect us, and the Yanks fly when and where they want,' I dared to say.

Sturmbannführer Walter Jokusch had downed a few drinks. 'Those Yankee planes,' he stammered. 'Who would be surprised? Goering would rather screw his movie stars than look after the Luftwaffe. What an inept fatso! He didn't take care of Stalingrad back then, and soon he'll be out of planes.'

What astonished me was that the entire party agreed with Jokusch, without explicitly stating it. So this is what it had come down to, I reasoned. Everyone anticipated the downfall, and everyone was seeking someone to blame for it.

Looking around, I realized I was the group's youngest and shortest member. They all paid close attention to my stories. Still, none of those wimps would have wanted to be in my shoes! I told them about my jeep, which we had captured, and how I had placed wounded Yanks on the bonnet to avoid the Americans shooting at me. I told them about the drugs recovered from the Americans, which were highly prized, above all the penicillin.

At this point, the thirty-five-year-old SS Hauptsturmführer and doctor Walter Pöschl interjected, saying, 'Listen, comrades, I have information from a reliable source that they gave our Führer American penicillin following the assassination attempt on him four months ago at the Wolf's Lair. If only the Yanks knew!' Pöschl, like Walter Jokusch, was in charge of a course at the SS Medical Academy. He was a ruddy-faced chap, Austrian-born, and had joined the Party before the Anschluss, but he was not politically active.

'My Hauptsturmführer,' Schlink said as he poured himself his fifth glass of red wine, 'this is no secret amongst us doctors. Next time, Herr Untersturmführer, remember to bring a tiny pack of those penicillin ampoules!' he added, turning to me.

I went on with my report. 'During the retreat to the West Wall, we had to advance again towards the US Army to save a Division of the Wehrmacht from a hopeless situation. Our Waffen SS spared thousands from certain death.'

'Of course, the Wehrmacht! If they fought like us, we would already have won the war,' remarked Helmut Ehrlinger. For a while we discussed the elite position of the Waffen SS.

'Venereal diseases are on the decline,' I continued. 'We come into less contact with friendly civilians now.'

'Yes, but you can look at that positively,' Martin remarked.

'You don't have to be concerned about your wife,' Horst added. 'Mother and childcare function well wherever she has fled, important now as the war is raging. Isn't her family at St. Pölten in Lower Danube?'

Helmut Ehrlinger stepped in and turned to face me, saying, 'I agree, Herr Untersturmführer, a young German woman with a small child, they're our future. Help is on the way. Your son will have the good fortune to find his destiny in the glorious new German Fatherland.'

I went back to my lodgings and went to bed distraught. What a bizarre, strange, and surreal experience! Would we still be able to win the war with folks like this on our side? That seemed unlikely. What to do? Only one thought came to mind…

RESI

I still had two days left of my leave when I arrived at Resi's Sporgasse Lane apartment. We hadn't spoken to one another in over five years, and I hoped this meeting would help me decide what to do.

Resi opened the door. 'I've come to visit you,' I said. Hiding her surprise, but not her apprehension, she invited me in. 'Remove your uniform jacket and leave your cap and satchel in the corridor. It's cold in here, so I'll lend you one of Karl's heavy jumpers.'

The stove supplied little warmth in the kitchen, where we sat at the table. 'There are no briquettes to collect from the cellar,' she added, smiling. She paused thoughtfully before continuing, 'I am alone in the flat. My husband is fighting on the Eastern Front and Karl is on the Italian front in the south. My son is only nineteen years old! I'm hoping he'll do the right thing and defect to the Americans. But if I utter something like that outside, I'll be hanged from the nearest lamp post with a sign around my neck reading "Doubted the Final Victory". That's what it's come to!

'Oh, Resi, we haven't talked in a long time. A student friend of mine fell pregnant, and I was duty-bound to marry her. My son is two years old now. My Division lies along the West Wall and I got special leave to care for my wife and child after the bombing of Graz, but I haven't been able find them. She escaped to the West because she was scared of the Russians. I wanted to meet up with you before I return to the front.'

Schlossberg, Graz

I reflected on the summer of 1939, more than five years earlier, when I had visited Resi after a long break. Although Karl had been pleased to see me, Resi had not. She had seen me roaming around town with young women the previous year and had been disappointed that I had forgotten about her so quickly. She'd taken an interest in hearing my plans, though, and had cautioned me strongly against joining the Waffen SS. 'Stay away from them. You extend your small finger, and they take your entire hand. This will not end well.' Despite giving a great deal of thought to her advice, I joined up two months later.

Resi played a soul album, and a black soloist began to sing. 'I haven't listened to music in a long time. I've been depressed. I adored you, I wanted to escape with you to a Sicilian mountain village, where we could relax on a balcony in the sun and eat tomatoes drenched in olive oil.' She placed her warm hand softly on my shoulder and looked into my eyes. That was all it took. We ripped off our clothes, and she dragged me into the bedroom.

Later on we lay there, exhausted but content, only this time we both smoked a cigarette. 'You're older,' Resi said, 'but I'm delighted nothing has changed.' And, with a smile, she added, 'At least not what's between your legs. You were lucky. That grenade could have blown off more than you bargained for.'

We were now matched – equals. I had outgrown my teen years and had lived through the war. Resi was lovely – natural, casual and laid-back. They say you never forget your first love, but it was more than that! Although she was fifteen years my senior, we were like soul mates.

She went shopping with my food stamps. We smoked the cigarettes keyt in my backpack and drank water and pear schnapps while she cooked for us. What time we had left together, we spent in bed. At the end of the second day, I dressed once again in my SS uniform.

I stood in the dark hallway. Resi didn't come to the door; instead she leaned against the cooker and said, 'Look after yourself, Sepp, and be sure to make the right decision!'

'Please wait for me, Resi,' I said, quietly opening the door, 'and I'll take you to Sicily, where we'll live for the rest of our lives.' And then I left, distraught, closing the door behind me.

Those two days had prompted me to reflect. Resi had intimated I should defect to the Americans, though she hadn't openly said so. Was that because she feared for my life or for hers?

After the war, I searched for Resi in vain. Had her husband and son both come back from the war? Was she expecting me in Sicily? It may sound sentimental, but some people can be overcome by a great love, it's a force that draws people to each other. It happened to me and I still sense the pain of losing it today.

I never mentioned Resi during the American interrogations or in my responses to the Moral Questionnaire. My marriage to Gretl had to be viewed as a sincere love match, and you are now the only person who knows anything about Resi.

She was the most enriching woman I've ever loved. We were powerfully drawn to each other. I was twenty-three years old when we last met, and she was thirty-eight, but still today, she remains my ideal woman.

DECISION

As the train from Graz to Cologne roared relentlessly towards the front, I had time to reflect on my life, questioning whether I was partly to blame for the predicament of my fellow humans. Resi had given me the Louis Pasteur birthday speech years before: 'Whether or not fate favors a man's work, at the end of his life, he should be able to say to himself, "I have done what I could".' Had I?

An older man sat across from me, engrossed in his book, from which he sometimes glanced up. He seemed unconcerned by my SS uniform. Only a week before, on my way to Graz, I'd had quite a different experience with a couple in their forties, who reacted with obvious hostility to my presence. But I had learned to live with such feelings and reactions. The next battle was looming. It was time to consider my choices.

What had happened to my life goals and the freedom I believed I would have to choose my own path? I had been in an institution, the Catholic seminary, with the Franciscans when I first decided to lead a different life. Yet now, I was back in the grips of another institution, the Waffen SS, where I had to do as they told me. From the frying pan into the fire, from one straitjacket to the next! When would I be able to live my life the way I wanted?

I began my medical studies five years ago. I had been content and enjoyed learning, but it had only lasted three months; followed by gunnery training, the French invasion, and several military schools, all of which interfered with my medical studies. Later on, again at the SS Medical Academy, I was subjected to semi-annual evaluations, during which my commander objected to my unsuitable lifestyle. True, while at the Academy, I received free lodging and an officer's salary, but that was it.

I would not have attended university or military schools if I had not joined the SS. But, in the end, I would still have found myself fighting at the front. Regardless of all my soul-searching, I was now on my way back to a battlefield, where I might well end up as fresh cannon fodder for the US Air Force! Had I been a zealous Nazi, I would have believed in an ideal I was willing to die for. But I'd never been one of those fanatics, loyal to the very last breath. All I wanted was to survive... was that too much to ask? My first war wound had not affected me too badly, but what about the next?

A soldier's life did not suit me at all; now that the carefree and youthful joy had passed, the extreme seriousness of my situation was slowly dawning. It wasn't the prospect of dying young that bothered me; it was also the fact that I could not influence my own life and death. A soldier must obey orders. There could be no arguments about it. The only thing that mattered was one's military rank and the number of stars on one's collar. Resi had urged me not to join hierarchical organizations where freedom would be curtailed. She could easily give such advice, though. I couldn't just resign from the army. I was up to my neck in shit. And I despised military life.

**Salmutter family: Gretl, Sepp Salmutter and Herwig,
December 1943**

And then there was Gretl. I had a wife and a child to consider, something I'd never planned. Gretl would limit my freedom, no matter what the future held, I thought, as the train rumbled toward the Western front.

During my visit, I had got along well with my uncle, but not with my grandmother. She was 73 years old, fragile, and ill. Years of hard labor had left her with a bent back. I didn't have any brothers or sisters, cousins, or aunts – only a childless uncle. My grandmother's only hope for a descendant was me. We had never time to build a loving bond, due to her age and the demands of labor on the farm from early morning until late at night. My move to the Franciscan seminary at the age of ten hadn't helped our situation. Still, she had raised me, and I felt a strong attachment to her.

It was always difficult for me to commit emotionally to anyone. I'm not sure if this was due to circumstance, genetics, or a combination of both. Whatever the case, it was hard for me to get into my grandmother's mind and understand her way of thinking.

Now I had other worries. I was about to face the worst battle of my life.

BATTLE OF THE BULGE AND DESERTION

Serving in the 2nd SS Panzer Division Das Reich, I participated in the Ardennes offensive, which is still glorified today as the Germans' last stand against a many times mightier enemy. Upon returning from Graz, I was promoted to SS Obersturmführer, equivalent to First Lieutenant, sporting three stars and a silver bar on my collar.

Germany had lost the naval and air wars. The Allies had complete air supremacy at the front and over the Reich's territory. After severe setbacks on land over the last months, could the fate of the Third Reich still be turned around? I had my doubts.

Some 200,000 German soldiers advanced through the hilly Ardennes countryside running along the Belgian-German frontier. We were to cut off the Anglo-American forces from their rear bases as far as southern Holland. Hitler planned to drive a wedge between the British and American Divisions by crossing the Meuse River in two days, recapturing within seven days the port of Antwerp, which harbored Allied supplies, and reaching the Atlantic coast in ten days. Brussels would be conquered and liberated and Allied forces were to be captured or destroyed. Hitler, who supervised the planning and execution of the offensive, relied on the lousy weather, forcing enemy bombers to stay grounded.

Back home, the domestic political situation was geared toward a total war effort. It came down to mobilizing every last human, material and moral force available. With his talent for oratory, Propaganda Minister Joseph Goebbels gave fiery speeches to strengthen the German peoples' resilience with a mixture of threats, promises, lies, and half-truths. 'We will win the final victory!' Goebbels had screamed in the Berlin sports stadium.

Like the 1940 campaign, our armored units were to make their way through the Eiffel Mountains and the rough terrain of the Ardennes to drive back the enemy forces. Four SS Panzer Divisions – 'Leibstandarte SS Adolf Hitler,' 'Das Reich,' 'Hohenstaufen,' and 'Hitler Youth' – were on stand-by south-west of Cologne.

The Allies had assessed the German offensive capability in the winter of 1944/45 as negligible and did not anticipate a German counter attack. The Brits' Field Marshal Mont-gomery planned to fly back home to spend Christmas with his family, while in Paris, on December 16, the US Com-mander-in-Chief Dwight Eisenhower was relaxing with a game of golf.

However, it was on this day, December 16, 1944, that the German offensive would begin. Fog and clouds covered the border area of Germany, Luxembourg, and Belgium. In addition, it was snowing intermittently. Early morning, our artillery fire started on a broad front as we moved across winding forest tracks and frozen fields. We progressed through villages which had been under Prussian, French, Flemish, and German administrations over the last 150 years. The farmers who had stayed on their land spied for us. We called them 'Rucksack Germans.'

My Division fought in the area of Gouvy – known by Germans as Geilich – and La Roche-en-Ardenne. I did not know of Hitler's strategy and was merely one of two hundred thousand bodies in uniform. This horrible war was not my war; I did my best to patch up the wounded and help save lives.

At first, we advanced well. The infantry and tanks led the advance, and we followed the troops with a mobile field hospital and all-terrain vehicles. Three of us sat in a Red Cross vehicle – the driver was an eighteen-year-old fanatical fellow from Mecklenburg, then there was a twenty-year-old medical assistant who had recently joined the SS, and me, a doubting twenty-three-year-old SS Obersturmführer.

A relentless and dirty war began in the confined space of the forest terrain. Tanks shot at tanks; both sides fired bazookas and anti-tank grenades. Snipers shot from treetops at any moving or crawling enemy. Men fought close to one another, often hiding between trees. The brutality did not end on the killing fields. Much later, I learned there had been an SS massacre in Malmedy, where the Germans shot 84 captured Americans who had been trying to escape.

As the German High Command had hoped, the horrible weather held during the initial days of the offensive. On December 19, 1944, our tanks rolled towards the Meuse River, bypassing the town of Bastogne. Heavy artillery fire and a subsequent infantry breakthrough followed the tank advance.

We trapped the American 106th Infantry Division in the snow-covered Eiffel Mountains east of St. Vith. Under massive fire from our forces, confused and inexperienced US officers panicked and tried to retreat. We continued to fire with all our available guns. In between assaults, we played the music of Benny Goodman, Artie Shaw and other American bandleaders from huge loudspeakers. Between the musical numbers, we added promises of *'showers, warm beds, and hotcakes for breakfast... if you surrender'*.

And this psychological warfare is what the frightened Americans succumbed to. One of their officers waved a white snow uniform and approached our front line to deliver their surrender. We captured eight thousand Americans and made them prisoners. It was one of the largest surrenders in American military history.

Apart from taking American soldiers out of action, their surrender meant a valuable addition to our resources, in the form of equipment. I got an American Jeep; the three of us used it to collect the wounded, both Germans and Americans, and take them to the military hospital.

In the following days, however, our tanks did not succeed in bypassing St. Vith and faced fierce Allied resistance. Nevertheless, on the evening of December 19, we understood than the situation for the Allied forces had significantly deteriorated.

There were no American forces anywhere within a twenty-mile-wide southern gap at Bastogne. Our tanks took advantage of this situation and rolled on towards the

Meuse River and the town of Namur, which was undefended. Our infantrymen surrounded Bastogne itself.

The surprise attack seemed to have succeeded. However, on the fifth day of the battle, we could not overpower the heavily defended Bastogne transport hub, where the Americans stored three million gallons of fuel, a prize we desperately needed as our own resources dwindled.

A traffic jam near St. Vith blocked us. To move forward, we had to swerve to the south. Due to a lack of fuel, we got delayed for a day. Miscalculations and supply breakdowns can happen in any war. Unknown terrain, unpredictable weather, failed communication links, vehicles driven over mines, and the unpredictability of the enemy all play a decisive role in the victory. And even the best-laid plans can get defeated.

On December 22, a thin layer of snow fell again, but unfortunately, the sky cleared, and the Americans began massive air attacks on our positions and tanks. Two corps of General Patton's army opened a powerful thrust at Celles, bringing our offensive to a halt only five kilometers from the Meuse River. Moreover, a few days later, Patton's men succeeded in breaking through the siege ring around Bastogne, which they had been defending and supplying from the air.

The nights were freezing. At the medical station, we were soon treating more cases of frostbite than war wounds. Wearing wet clothes and socks in cold temperatures and a damp climate caused painful frostbites on fingers and toes.

What could we do when there was no way to dry them? Whenever possible, we put on warm dry clothes looted from the Americans.

Toward the end of the war, a new drug became a game-changer for medics. Penicillin meant wounds and infections could be treated and cured. The Allies had it, and it revolutionized their medical treatment. Sepsis, or blood poisoning, was no longer a killer. The drug saved tens of thousands of Americans, but to our deep frustration we had no access to it. Our only supplies were what we could capture from the Americans.

It was sunny over Christmas week, and no snow fell. The nights were cold, and the daytime temperatures stayed around freezing. The overall Allied air superiority hampered the ground operations of the German army. Our advance towards the Meuse River failed to materialize due to General Patton's army's massive defense operation. Our acute fuel shortage became a significant hindrance.

At 03:00 am on Christmas Day, our front section attacked again. By daybreak, we had made two breaches. However, the eighteen German tanks that had broken through were soon blown up, and the infantry suffered heavy losses.

The battle was brutal, with fanatical fighters on both sides. By the afternoon of Christmas Day, the Americans had restored their front line. The slaughter continued the next day, and we were still short on fuel.

The day before New Year's Eve, the weather deteriorated, as we had hoped. Light snow fell at first, but from January 7 onward, there was heavy snowfall. A severe frost over the next few days hampered operations on both sides.

In early January, six Divisions of Patton's army, led by their swashbuckling commander, attacked in the vicinity of Bastogne. To fight his troops, the Germans brought four armored Divisions from the north wing of the offensive to the south. The ensuing battle on the 3rd and 4th of January was the fiercest and most costly of the entire offensive. New and inexperienced soldiers in both German and American Divisions were the likely cause. On January 5, our onslaught began to wane, and the Allies resumed their attack.

The Americans made slow progress in their counter-offensive, as the dense fog had made air support impossible. Our soldiers had lost their fear of enemy tanks. In the forest, they could sneak up close to the Americans, putting their tanks out of action using piercing grenades. Using the 'stovepipe,' a rocket-powered anti-armor rifle, so-called because of its shape and the smoke it produced when fired, the Germans destroyed US tanks from a manageable distance. As soon as a tank was out of action, traffic flow stalled, the roads being too narrow to get past the wreckage.

On January 19, a snowstorm raged in the Ardennes. The past month had taken its toll on me both physically and mentally, and I had come to see the futility of this slaughter. Fallen men lay frozen stiff in the snow. Many of the soldiers we picked up did not survive another day. I became desperate. Five weeks earlier, the battle had not started so badly for me, but now everywhere I looked, there were corpses. The thought of escape grew stronger.

> 'In October 1944, POW frequently listened to a program, "Sendungen für Österreich," sponsored by the Allied radio station in LUXEMBURG. For a long time, POW had nursed the desire to quit the SS and fight for Austria. After hearing these programs, POW decided to be on the alert for an opportunity to desert.' [Curriculum vitae]

I decided to take the first opportunity to desert to the other side. After our forces had massacred French civilians and partisans in southern France, and shot captured Americans at Malmedy, I was uncertain what would happen to me once I defected to the Americans. Furthermore, if my escape failed, my own Division would summarily execute me.

How could I best break away from the German troops? Where and how would I hide? What would I say to the Americans to avoid being shot straightaway? I guessed they might be no less forgiving with their prisoners than the Germans had been. Resi's quotes from Pasteur's speech started to make more sense. 'Let us be able to say, when near to the end of life, "I have done what I could".' I no longer thought about my oath to Adolf Hitler. The will to survive had become too great.

On January 20, 1945, the opportunity to desert finally arose.

> 'I had learned of our infantry's withdrawal and decided to leave the Division's command post at Beho. The danger of escape was palpable as the battle was raging all around me. I set off under cover of chaos and darkness, sneaking about 3 miles forward, through our infantry and on terrain ideal for hiding mines, toward the Americans at Gouvy.' [Curriculum vitae]

Jan 21, 1945: Gouvy is captured by the US Army.
Salmutter reports to the US forces and becomes Prisoner-of-War

I had to be extremely careful because of the mines we had laid. I paused to catch my breath and listen in the surrounding darkness, trying to determine where my Division and the enemy's had moved to. I had to find a place to hide – and soon. All would fall into place, one way or another, I hoped. Finding a dilapidated hunter's shack at the edge of the forest, I decided to hide there.

The German army had retreated, and the 1st US Army took Gouvy. Once I was confident the Americans had conquered the territory, I ventured out of cover and surrendered. That is how on January 21, 1945, I ended up in captivity.

> *'I was wearing a US Army shirt and shoes when I was captured.'*
> *[Curriculum vitae]*

The above entry is in the US files, but still, to this day, I can't remember or explain it. Maybe I had put them on to avoid being shot at by the Americans? Was this from loot we had got hold of earlier?

While in captivity, I had ample time to think about whether my desertion was against my oath to the Führer. Would my defection absolve me from the evil in which I had taken part, or would I still have to pay for my deeds later?

Whilst I was being interrogated by the Americans, the Battle of the Bulge continued. By February 1945, the Germans had lost all areas gained to the Allied counter-offensive. In total, more than one million soldiers had taken part in this battle. For the USA, the Battle of the Bulge was the bloodiest land battle of the Second World War, resulting in around twenty thousand casualties.

The number of deaths on the German side was more than seventeen thousand.

To complete the history of the Panzer Division Das Reich: after the failed Ardennes offensive, in March 1945, the Division, together with other SS Divisions, transferred to Hungary, where it remained until the end of the war. It took part in Operation Spring Awakening against the advancing Red Army.

My service in the SS Panzer Division Das Reich was limited to the French/Belgium/Holland campaigns in the summer of 1940, where no fighting took place, the French/Belgian campaign in the summer and autumn of 1944, and the subsequent Battle of the Bulge in 1944/45. I served as a medic in all three battles. In November 1944, I was promoted to Obersturmführer, equivalent to a Staff Doctor. Above me in rank were the Oberstabsarzt, Generalarzt, Generalstabsarzt, and Generaloberststabsarzt.

Herwig, at this point, I close an unpleasant chapter of my life – my pact with National Socialism and the Waffen SS. While growing up under the Nazis, my views had changed. I know I didn't always do the 'right' thing, but I didn't always know what the 'right' thing was. With age and hindsight, however, one becomes wiser.

While writing about the Battle of the Bulge, I remembered our head-to-head chat in October a year ago, when you stayed for two days with me in Germany and told me about your 'war experiences' in Biafra. Though I did not do so at the time, I must now set you straight.

BIAFRAN WAR

You had come back from a year working on oil rigs in West Africa. Of the many stories you told me, I was most interested in your account of the war in Biafra. I could draw parallels to the Second World War, not knowing then that I would experience yet another war in Vietnam. When you spoke of your war experiences, I was not yet prepared to tell you mine on the Western Front. I could only smile at your 'courage,' your bravado, and your arrogance. You meant well, but you had no clue what real war was about.

What was your war like? In 1967, after you had been in Dahomey for six months, Schlumberger Oil Services transferred you to Nigeria. Biafra wanted to secede from Nigeria, and the conflict had claimed a million lives. Pictures of starving children on television and in the papers were haunting. After the Biafran military forces conquered Port Harcourt, your company moved its headquarters to Warri in the Niger Delta. You never worked in Biafra itself. Schlumberger was a subcontractor for Shell, which meant you had access to all the facilities a powerful Western company could provide, such as a supermarket, medical care, cinema, and tennis courts.

The oil rigs were close to the front line, you explained. At checkpoints, young, trigger-happy black boys armed with sub-machine guns stopped your Landrover for inspection. They were as scared of you as you were of them. They searched your car and grabbed a shirt or towel, always with the machine gun pointed at you. You were not afraid.

Herwig Salmutter with friends in West Africa, 1967

Instead, you felt sympathy and understanding for the black population, which had only a few years ago obtained independence from Britain.

The Biafran war had blown up most of the bridges, and your Landrover had to cross rivers on temporary ferries. One night, hungry Biafran soldiers stormed the food container on the drilling rig drilling in the middle of the jungle. You slept through the episode, not noticing anything was amiss. Six months later, the insurgents killed eleven Italians on the same rig. Luckily, by then you were doing your job somewhere else.

Your war… my ass! Do you call this war? Is this what you think living through a war means? Opposite your flats, there was a disco with nice-looking young black girls, remember? You bought them drinks and gave them money for the taxi fare home. Now and then, you slept with them and called it 'girlfriend experience.' When you came back at night from a job lasting several days, you would some-times find a black girl in your bed because in bad weather, with torrential rain pelting down, your house boy would let her sleep over. Being young and unattached, you liked the girls. You got the clap, and you got crabs, like we did in our times. To treat the clap, a nurse stuck a needle into your bum in a domino 'five' pattern over five consecutive days; she had a sense of humor. You enjoyed your job, and you earned a lot.

You were 24 years old; I was 23 during the Battle of the Bulge, but we lived through different war conditions. Your recruitment requirements were to be under 28, single, fit for the tropics, have a university degree, complete a company training course, and sign up for a one-year overseas contract without leave. The American Hospital in Cluny in Paris checked your tropical fitness. Only half the candidates passed the two-month training – those who made it felt elite and were willing to sell their souls for the company.

My recruitment criteria were different; for the Waffen SS, one had to be at least 17 years of age, 1.72 m tall (a barrier for some southern Germans), healthy, single, and possess a positive attitude toward National Socialism. A high school degree was not necessary. My schools were the SS Military Academies in Tölz and Braunschweig.

You experienced your 'war' as an adventure, working with engineers from America, England, France, and Switzerland. In the SS, we were all Germans, and there was a high chance of being killed, becoming nothing more than a number on the daily casualty list. I was lucky to have only got shrapnel in my thigh.

In this final part of my autobiography, I want to share my remaining time in American captivity and also write about my life in post-war Austria, East, and West Germany. First, however, let me go back to Fort Hunt in the State of Virginia, where the Yanks had interned and interrogated me.

TRANSLATION SERVICE – HIRED

After three weeks in America and extensive questioning, I was ordered to stay and serve for another nine months in their Fort Hunt Translation Service, rather than being sent to a POW camp somewhere out in the vastness of the United States. The Americans wanted me to work for them because I understood English well and I could translate all the army jargon, which was incomprehensible to civilian German-speakers. I felt appreciated and liked my new job. The food was good, the hours fixed, and I dressed in a US Army uniform. I had to salute casually with two fingers, and thus, unexpectedly, found myself serving on the opposing side! I assisted in the translation of secretly eavesdropped discussions of German POWs. I didn't think twice, didn't hesitate, and adapted to my new circumstances.

Finally, the motives behind the secret eavesdropping and the detainees' interrogations became clear to me. The Americans wanted to find out how deeply Nazi ideology had poisoned the minds of Wehrmacht and SS soldiers; they wanted to know how the German civilian population – our family, relatives, and friends – would feel about them occupying postwar Germany and Austria.

All senior American interrogation officers had to speak German. Only people who knew German as their mother tongue could transcribe and read the interrogation protocols. Prisoners often mumbled or spoke in dialect.

In the main it was immigrant German Jews who copied the interrogations and eavesdropped on conversations.

REPORT OF INTERROGATION NO. 5102

N: SALMUTTER, Sepp
R: Obersturmfuehrer
U: I./SS Pz Arty Regt "Das Reich"
C: 21 Jan '45, GOUVY, Belgium

Date: 20 April 1945.
I/O : Capt. Brown

PREAMBLE:

P/W is a wide-awake, intelligent, young Austrian who joined the SS so he could attend the SS Medical Academy in his home town of GRAZ and thus continue his studies. He is violently anti-Nazi and most reliable. His typically Austrian behavior, his marriage to a non-Aryan, and, finally, his desertion to the Americans secured for him a dishonorable discharge and death sentence, or, in other words: "Verurteilung zum Tode mit Ausstoss aus der SS mit Schimpf und Schande"

REPORT OF INTERROGATION NO. 5102

N: Salmutter, Sepp
R: Obersturmfuehrer

Date: 20 April 1945
I/O: Capt. Brown

U: I./SS Pz Arty Regt "Das Reich"
C: 21 Jan '45, GOUVY, Belgium

SECRET

P/W is a wide-awake, intelligent, young Austrian who joined the SS so he could attend the SS Medical Academy in his home town of GRAZ and thus continue his studies. He is violently anti-Nazi and most reliable. His typically Austrian behavior, his marriage to a non-Aryan, and, finally, his desertion to the Americans secured for him a dishonorable discharge and death sentence, or, in other words: "Verurteilung zum Tode mit Ausstoss aus der SS mit Schimpf und Schande"

Sepp Salmutter is classified as 'most reliable' and was ordered to stay and serve for another nine months in the Fort Hunt Translation Service.

When German POWs said something vital, a good eaves-
dropper would know. A notice on the listening station's
wall read, 'When in doubt, push the button RECORD.'
They taped what they heard and later transcribed it on
paper.

QUESTIONNAIRE

In October 1945, after six months of duty in the Translation Service, I was ordered to compose essays about my views and experiences, as well as my hopes and anxieties for the future. These notes were to form a more extensive report than the Moral Questionnaire I had filled out after arriving at Fort Hunt in April. They handed me particular questions to answer and topics to write about, and I was given a two-week break to prepare my answers.

The fighting had ended, the German Wehrmacht had surrendered in May, and Japan likewise in August, after the US detonated nuclear bombs over Hiroshima and Nagasaki. Germany and Austria became two independent countries divided into Allied occupation zones. They suffered from periods of famine and housing shortages. The Russians had made inroads into Central and Eastern Europe, including Germany and Austria, while the other Allies – the Americans, British, and French took the Western side.

I was twenty-four years old; I had studied medicine but was also interested in history and economics. I felt honored to be asked for my thoughts on the questions put before me but who would, I wondered, want to read my report? How far up the chain would it go? Would copies be circulated? After January 1945, American newspapers were my only source of information about global affairs and they were biased because victors, of course, always write their own history. I would try to compose my essays based on how I saw the world from my perspective.

Looking back thirty years later at what I wrote, on the one hand, I feel proud, and on the other, I find some of it to be naïve and poorly thought out. But how could I have known anything different in 1945? Herwig, I do not wish to conceal from you the opinions I held at that time. Please note that all quotes from US Intelligence documents are *in italic font.*

Historical events that precipitated WWII

Following World War I, the Treaties of Versailles and Saint-Germain in 1919 were humiliating for Germany and Austria and destructive for both economies. Today, most historians accept that the survival of emerging republics and democracies was challenging under these conditions. The rise of Hitler was, to a large extent, a result of the harsh 1919 peace treaties.

'However, one must distinguish between the fundamental and the more immediate causes of the war. The deeper causes of both this war and the First World War stemmed from the tensions between the industrial and progressive Central European countries on the one hand and the agricultural and conservative Eastern European countries on the other — most notably the tensions between Germany and Russia. One must not forget the pan-Slavic destabilizing activity before the First World War.

As far as the immediate causes of the war are concerned, Hitler was guilty of not having tried to solve the problems through negotiation. Germany's decision to go to war, especially against Russia, with which it had had good relations, was sudden and risky, fueled by the tremendous arrogance of the Nazi leaders.

The Weimar Republic was designed to become a true democracy. Parliament could have gradually resolved its shortcomings had it not been for the severe economic conditions forced on Germany after the First World War.'

SECRET

Report of Interrogation :   5 November 1945
                                                        I/O : Capt. HALLE
P/W   : SALMUTTER, Sepp
Rank   : 1st Lt. SS
Unit   : 1 Obt.Pz.Arty.Regt.Das Reich
Captd : Gouvy/Belgium, 21 January 1945.

Veracity : Believed reliable.

Report : Answers to Questionaire submitted by Propaganda Branch 23 October 1945.

Note : Before answering the questionaire, P/W wants to emphasize that he is an
Austrian, 25 years of age and that he therefore will discuss the Austrian
situation. It can generally be likened to Germany's situation of today, however,
except for nominal and insignificant differences.

SECRET

Report of interrogation: 5 November 1945

I/O: Capt.HALLE

P/W   :   SALMUTTER Sepp
Rank   :   1st Lt. SS
Unit   :   1 Obt.Pz.Art.Reg.Das Reich
Captd: Gouvy/Belgium, 21 January 1945.

Veracity: Believed reliable.

Report : Answers to Questionnaire submitted by Propaganda Branch 13 Oct 1945

Note : Before answering the questionnaire, P/W wants to emphasize that he is an Austrian, 25 years of age and that he therefore will discuss the Austrian situation. It can generally be likened to Germany's situation of today, however, except for nominal and insignificant differences.

Sepp Salmutter was ordered to complete a detailed questionnaire on military and political issues and visions of the future

Hitler's fight against Bolshevism

Hitler desired to safeguard Europe from Bolshevism and hoped that his war against Russia would garner support throughout Europe. He did, however, start the war too soon. Earlier, I stated that I did not regard my instruction at the SS Military Academies as education in the traditional sense but rather as an experience. In retrospect, I believe that the National Socialist brainwashing I received stopped me from understanding just how far Western Europe would have gone to oppose Bolshevism. After the end of the war, I remained trapped in the National Socialist mindset.

'Throughout Europe, people widely feared Bolshevism. Russia is a large country and was building a mighty army. Germany had tried to prevent the Bolsheviks from gaining a foothold in Europe for a long time. Hitler perhaps dreamed of becoming Europe's savior from Bolshevism. In Hitler's eyes, the Nazi conquest of other European countries was the precondition for a successful war against the alleged expansionist efforts of Bolshevik Russia. Hitler's attempts to convince European countries to join the Germans in challenging Russia had only been partially successful.

The threat that Hitler saw in Russia did not yet exist, and all his speculations may have been similarly unfounded. He imposed his will on millions of Europeans by launching the war, taking away their freedom to run their own countries. Germans became hated oppressors in foreign lands, even though many non-communists throughout Europe had initially supported Hitler's Germany. It was Hitler who started the war but, had it been the Bolsheviks who launched attacks against the rest of non-communist Europe, Germany would have become a welcome ally in defense of Europe from communism. Despite the political, economic, and ethnological tensions between Eastern and Western Europe, war should not have been the means to resolve them. I now see this war as a conflict arising from economic conditions and moral issues.'

A democratic Germany
would not have started a war

'Germans, as a rule, are a peace-loving people. Had the Germans lived in a democracy when the war began, that is to say, had they understood the actual international situation, they would not have gone to war.

During the Kaiser's reign and before, politicians told the German people to believe that war was an inevitable fact of international politics, as in Clausewitz's statement: "War is politics by other means." Germany's Nazi leadership is responsible for the war. They aroused nationalistic passions through their successful propaganda campaigns, leading Germans to believe that when conflicts arise, "to attack is the best form of defense," thus making the cruelty of warfare acceptable.'

The role of the Catholic Church before the war

'The most influential clergyman is undoubtedly the parish priest who has direct contact with the people. In Austria, the clergy draws its members primarily from the sons of farmers and workers; sons of the upper classes seldom join the clerical hierarchy. I had been a typical example: as a bright orphan, I was destined to become a parish priest at the expense of the church.'

Underground movements against Hitler

'It is unlikely that the Social Democrats cooperated with other underground movements. The fear of getting lured into fictitious covert activities secretly led by the Gestapo – the secret police service – was too great. Only party members who knew each other well met in secret.

Over time, the Communist underground movement expanded into a radical anti-Nazi force. Many Germans sympathized with this movement, and the opposition to continuing the war had become the main rallying point for anti-Nazi activists.

Former Communist Party members worked in the large industrial quarters. Members of other parties who did not come from the *working class were soon conscripted to military service. In contrast, communist workers who were needed for industrial production were allowed to stay longer in their places. Many workers in critical positions escaped conscription.*

The Communist Party, therefore, did not lose as many members to war and was consequently able to preserve its Party structure. These were die-hard opponents of the Nazis who remained true to their political views. They carried out their well- camouflaged but risky activities with far greater energy and success than members of other parties.'

Austrian nationalism

'Most Austrians who aspire to a free and independent Austria see themselves as opponents of communism. Indeed, the Austrian nationalists fought together with the Austrian communists to liberate Austria from the Nazis. Nevertheless, once liberated by Allied forces, they had achieved their common goal, after which nationalists and communists parted ways. Nationalists feared that a communist Austria would lose all independence and wind up under Russia's sphere of influence.'

Concentration camps

During my officer training, the SS ordered me to spend a few days each at the concentration camps of Dachau, Sachsenhausen, and Buchenwald. I refused offers of transfer from the Waffen SS to the branch of the SS operating in the camps, where I would have been forced to conduct medical research on inmates. After my detention, I gave the Americans "extensive information" about these concentration camps. I pretended I had only visited the camps for a few hours at a time to avoid additional grilling.

'I'm not aware of any concentration camps exclusively meant for Jews. Concentration camps held a wide variety of nationalities for various reasons. I visited the Dachau concentration camp near Munich in March 1941 and the Buchenwald concentration camp near Weimar

in March 1942 as part of a brief tour. However, during these short visits, the camp commander only revealed to me what stood in stark contrast to the actual conditions, of which I only later came to learn from first-hand witnesses as a POW in Namur.

There were a significant number of concentration camps. As the war stretched on, the Nazis established many new ones. The well-known ones are Dachau, Buchenwald near Weimar, Sachsenhausen near Berlin, Mauthausen near Linz, and Auschwitz in Upper Silesia.

A special group of the SS ran the camps. These SS members kept the worst of their atrocities strictly hidden. Within the SS, only a tiny group was complicit in the genuinely terrible crimes that had been committed.

Camp Commanders:

von Angelo, Dachau around 1935,

Oberführer von Baranowski, in Sachsenhausen, and Obergruppen-führer Eicke was instrumental in setting up concentration camps. The Austrian Social Democrats certainly looked forward to the return of their former leaders. The latter had been locked up in concentration camps for "security reasons" due to their leaders' anti-Nazi stand and organizational talents. The Social Democratic Party needed these men to rebuild and run their organization precisely because of these skills.'

Russian communists to obtain maximum control

'Russia secured political influence over Germany's future by organizing and supporting their German prisoners of war in the so-called "National Committee for a Free Germany." It is safe to assume that the "Eastern ally," Russia, successfully indoctrinated its prisoners through communist "re-education. Russian influence in Germany: At this critical and decisive point in time, the German communists, supported by Russia, could build a Soviet empire on German soil. The Russians will denounce the Western democratic "capitalist" powers for not helping Germany. The Russians might play on the same sentiments often expressed in the West: "Let the Germans stew in their own juices" or "Why should the United States play Father Christmas for Europe?

The Germans may not support communism, but they may unwittingly allow active communists planted inside today's political parties to lead their country. The communists have influence throughout Germany, so I fear that Germany might turn communist soon. I do not know whether the Americans will allow this to happen.

The present German situation is known to me only through the American press, but as things stand, I see Germany facing some serious threats. In my opinion, Russia will try to create a Red Germany, as was attempted in 1921. This would be Russia's first step towards controlling all of Europe. The Soviet government is pursuing a clear and ruthless purpose. One must look behind the veil in all their actions and not be deceived by appearances. Russian influence in Austria: A skillfully executed Russian occupation of Eastern Austria could turn the original antipathy toward Russians into sympathy. Increased Russian influence is a two-fold victory – for Austrian communism and worldwide Bolshevism.

The word "Bolshevism" still evokes fear among a significant part of the Austrian population. If, however, the occupying Russians behave contrary to the National Socialist's anti-Russian propaganda, this fear will diminish. With its following among the devout rural population, the Catholic Church has remained the counterweight to both communism and atheism.'

Germany's difficult path to democracy

'Due to their systematic indoctrination by Nazi propaganda, the German people have been rendered incapable of expressing free political thought or will. They have been forced to live, act, and think in a way that has made them politically immature. This is particularly true of young voters who have never experienced a multi-party system. However, I do think Germany could become a democracy. In general, the German people have the social and psychological foundation on which a re-education to democracy can be based. I think that democracy would be the best form of government for Germany. It is the only viable alternative to totalitarianism. However, totalitarianism will win if the attempt to restore democracy to Germany is not implemented correctly or if it is begun too late. The USA, in particular, as a strong *example and guarantor of authentic and genuine democracy, should not shirk its responsibility in fostering true world peace by hiding in "splendid isolation" and walking away from European problems. American democracy could be a workable model for Germany, but the real spirit of US democracy can only be instilled after a period of thorough and patient re-education. The occupying powers should examine a return to the political system of the Weimar Republic.'*

President Roosevelt's Four Freedoms

In 1945, as a POW, I was in a precarious situation, and it was advisable to gain sympathy from the Yanks by praising their democracy. I wanted to be seen as being on the "right side," which happened to be the American side. Today, I am convinced that democracy is the best foundation for governing a country and that the Nazi dictatorship was an aberration in German and Austrian history.

'Essential features of democracy are best found in the Four Freedoms, as the late President Roosevelt proclaimed in his speech to Congress on January 6, 1941: Freedom of speech, freedom of religion, freedom from want, and freedom from fear. Aspiring to these four freedoms in Germany and assisting the Germans in implementing them would move Germany toward genuine democracy.'

Austria's path to democracy

'After the war, one could imagine the Austrian state structure reverting to the former democratic republic of 1938. Before the war, conservative clerical circles in Austria strived for a monarchy under Otto von Habsburg, but this would probably be too costly for a small and poor Austria. A constitutional monarchy would only be possible if Austria could establish a close union with Hungary. It would be welcome from an economic point of view because Hungary, with its fertile agricultural areas, and Austria, with its strong industry but poor agriculture, could support each other. A new Habsburg monarchy could be conceived by uniting the Catholic German provinces of Bavaria and the Rhineland with Austria.'

Punishment of National Socialist crimes

The Nuremberg war crimes trials were in progress, and Nazi atrocities were being broadcast to the entire world. As a young, low-ranking officer who had only served at the front, I escaped punishment. My release from the POW camps and repatriation to Austria in 1947 equated to my de-facto denazification. I was now free to pursue a civilian career.

'The German people's contact with democracy after the German collapse caused, I believe, a great deal of disillusionment. Though the need to denazify is undeniable, judges must carry it out in a way that most Germans, who were promised freedom from Hitler's yoke, can accept. I feel that Germans must be informed about the criminal character of the Nazis, but continuing to label the entire German nation as criminal will only instill hatred. It would demonstrate that the victors do not understand the living conditions suffered in a dictatorship. German people must not conclude that the victors' aim is the destruction of Germany, or else denazification will not be successful. The victors stated that they had come as liberators, not conquerors.

Punishing Nazi Leaders

A just and severe punishment of Nazi leaders who led Germany into this terrible situation will be supported. The same applies to those guilty of violating the Geneva Convention during the war. Serious offenders must be liquidated*, and less severe cases should be punished in a penal camp with several years of hard labor. It must be brought to the public's attention how Hitler's Germany carried out a scorched earth policy in occupied countries, leaving behind nothing but death and destruction.
* executed

Punishing ordinary citizens:

A civilian who had been an ordinary member of the NSDAP, the Nazi party, and had perhaps been forced into it, and who has no criminal record, should be pardoned and allowed to remain in his professional position unless there is an untainted person to whom that position can be entrusted.

The victors should not bring the civil bureaucracy to a breaking point, or else Germans might doubt the goodwill of the occupation authorities. The Russians understand this problem better and have a more workable system in their occupation zone. They have liquidated the higher Nazis in their region without much ado and allowed lower-ranking party members to continue doing the necessary work they were trained for.

Punishing Party members:

Full-time Nazis, from district leaders upward, must be neutralized*. Group leaders who ran local offices and were often guilty of great injustices must be removed from their functions. Party membership in itself is not a criterion for being a Nazi, since in many cases, one had to join the Nazi Party to keep one's employment. However, those who joined the Party just to obtain a higher position without being qualified ought to be punished.

* executed

Punishing SS members:

The occupying administration must investigate members of the SS for personal crimes. They must impose severe punishments on SS members who worked in concentration camps. Members of the Waffen SS, especially frontline troops, must be investigated for atrocities and acts of violence on the front and in occupied territories.'

At the time of this writing, I was convinced that Waffen SS soldiers who had committed no war crimes should be denazified without delay.

Punishing SA leaders:

An investigation of each individual must take place. SA members — so-called Storm Troopers — were often dumb and harmless, as were NSKK members [NS-Motoring-corps, a paramilitary sub-organization of the NSDAP with over 500,000 members], NSFK members [NS-Pilots-corps, a paramilitary sub-organization of the NSDAP, parachutists, glider pilots, etc.], as was the NS-Women's League — everyday citizens without specific political ambitions.

Punishing Hitler Youth members:

Hitler Youth leaders who served as full-time activists must be punished. Younger Hitler Youth members should be re-educated, but their incorrigible should be neutralized*.'

* executed

Necessary Allied aid

The living conditions in Germany and Austria during the winters of 1945/46 and 1946/47 were abysmal. I was still in America and did not know about the disaster back home. My countrymen were fighting to stay alive in a horrible famine, in which the average daily diet fell to only 800 kilocalories per person. Austrian agricultural productivity had dropped by 60% compared to 1937. Hundreds of thousands of Austrian refugees and millions of Germans had been forced out of the Reich's previously inhabited Eastern provinces and required assistance.The United Nations Relief and Rehabilitation Administration provided Europe with food, medicine, seeds, fertilizer, and textiles. The United States supplied 70% of the products, although Canada, South America, Australia, and India all contributed. American Christian relief organizations and private individuals in the United States began sending care packages to Europe, with Germany receiving more than half of them. The US Navy transported these parcels, totaling 100 million, at no cost; these were standard parcels, each with ten days of supplies for "one hungry person in Europe." Later, when I returned to Austria, I felt profound gratitude to the American people and their government. The care packages, the Marshall Plan, and the kindness of the American occupiers left a strong, lasting impression. Hopefully, the Americans took my warnings in the questionnaire I had prepared in 1945 at the onset of the winter into account.

'Apart from my hope and wish that Germany will become a true democracy, I fear the terrible situation predicted for the winter in Germany may help the German communists gain popularity in the aftermath of this war. Germany will seek cooperation with and depend on those who offer long-term loans. This will enable Germany to rebuild itself and ward off communism. Inevitably, Germany will, to some extent, become dependent on the occupation forces. Most Germans are counting on aid from the USA

Mourning and prayer alone will not bring about a better future for radicalized workers, civil servants, and ordinary citizens who lost everything. They will move forward without much sentimentality, scoff at the Catholic faith, and cling above all to an organization giving them work and aid. If the church helps, people will respond to it and follow it. Otherwise, while the faithful are kneeling at church services, activists will meet in clubhouses and make radical plans to improve their lot in some other way.'

Global justice can prevent a new war

'Anti-war propaganda will not be successful unless there is an equitable distribution of the world's wealth. If, for instance, the standard of living in neighboring countries is four times that of one's own, it could arouse understandable envy. Envy leads to wars. A new war with atom bombs would wipe out all of human civilization. Therefore, famines that breed fear, greed, and hunger must not be tolerated anywhere in the world.

It is a scientific fact that the world can produce enough food and clothing for all. There must be a general rise in living standards, allowing all people to buy and sell goods and earn enough money for their needs. It should be shown that war is avoidable and that humanity can peacefully resolve conflicts of interest.

The Catholic Church in a New Austria

'The Austrian clergy took a strong stance against National Socialism, though the clergy had no option but to accept the Anschluss of Austria in 1938 by the German Reich. The church suffered under the National Socialist government and had to go along with enforced deals to avoid harsher treatment

In principle, none of the clergy members were close to the Nazis. Still, in a Catholic country where the local political leader was often the mayor, a member of the NSDAP, and a good churchgoer, the relationship between him and the priest was typically amicable.

The Austrian Catholic clergy will have to participate in the revival of a free Austria. There are already vital signs of resurgence in religious piety. During the war, women and older men at home grew increasingly concerned for their loved ones at the front and became devoted churchgoers. Now, the many fallen soldiers are being mourned all over the country. The entire German nation has been affected and continues to search for consolation. Undoubtedly, the church will be able to give strength to believers, referring to "divine justice and the necessary submission" of every man to "His divine will"; only the "far-sighted wisdom of God" knows why this terrible trial has befallen the German people.

The Higher and Lower clergy have enjoyed considerable prestige among believers in Austria. During the Nazi regime, the Higher church was almost wholly removed from public life. However, the Lower church — village and town priests, Catholic teachers in primary schools — remained popular with the people.'

The Christian Social Party

'was one of the strongest political parties in democratic Austria before the Anschluss. Its primary support base came from rural areas and medium-sized towns, i.e., peasants, artisans, and the bourgeoisie.

The Concordat concluded between the Nazis and Pope Pius XI will be ratified again in the new Austria. However, the government must remove all National Socialist legislation regarding religious instruction in public schools, marriage, divorce legislation, etc. The Christian Social Party must consider whether it would be advisable to separate state and church — that is, births, marriages, deaths, etc., should be administered by the state. In contrast, religious matters should be left to the church.'

The role of the bourgeoisie in reconstruction

I had miscalculated the post-war state of the bourgeoisie when I filled out the questionnaire in October of 1945. Despite the destruction of industries and tenements resulting from the war, the bourgeoisie still held enough property and capital to quickly return to its old wealth and power. Was my erroneous diagnosis just wishful thinking, a subconscious desire to see once well-connected people lose most of their assets?

'There is no doubt that there will be an essential change in the relationship between the capitalist bourgeoisie and the working class after the war. It will no longer be possible to speak of a blatant division between these two former classes. The war—above all, the destruction of large cities in aerial bombardments and the extreme inflation after the fighting—will blur the class differences between the rich and the poor.'

Development opportunities in the near future

'The worsening conditions in the occupied zones of Germany pose near-insoluble problems for the Allies. It could lead to a point where, after years of misery and catastrophic post-war conditions, the German people will tell themselves, "Hitler was right; it was not just him and his system the Allies wanted to destroy, but the Allies intended that Germans should never again be allowed to lead a dignified existence. The prospects for a better future under "democratic freedom" are bleak and may not seem achievable. Germans have never attained the democratic freedom they strove for after the First World War. Therefore, they might reject democracy and instead choose the opposite. "Not much more can be lost; perhaps something can be gained" might be their conclusion. Germans should never view Hitler as a national martyr—the government must prevent this at all costs.

German heavy industry should be nationalized and well supervised to bolster the coffers of the state finances, thereby relieving the smaller taxpayers. Large farms should stay since their owners employ the most advanced farming methods, but they should be taxed more than small farmers. If possible, to stay viable, Germany should remain a united country within the borders that existed in 1933; large areas are agricultural, and others industrial, and they need each other to prosper.'

Jews in the New Germany

In October 1945, I thought the word "Jew" would never again be acceptable. However, Jews themselves have insisted on keeping this term, and the word "Jew" is now accepted as a value-free expression.

'Jews should have the same rights as every German. The eradication of the term "Jew" being used in the racist sense should be attempted, as the German people have been indoctrinated against the term. For a long time, this word alone will cause prejudice against a person labeled as such.

As far as expelled or deported Jews are concerned, I believe they should be entitled to return to Austria.

Regarding the expropriation of Jewish assets: All Jews who suffered under the Nazi regime should come forward to point the finger at those who enriched themselves from their Jewish possessions. I have no further knowledge of Jewish matters.'

My attitude towards the United States

I wrote the response below before transferring to Columbus, Wisconsin, where I had the opportunity to socialize with more Americans:

'When I think of America, the first thing that comes to mind is that it is a country where people can live in a truly human way. Thus far, I have formed my image of the United States through reading. My status as a prisoner-of-war has limited my contact with Americans. In my opinion, the best description of the United States is a world power where people have freedom of choice.'

About myself

'I do not believe that I was entirely cut off from important international news under the Nazi regime, as I did manage to listen to foreign broadcasts. I want to be kept informed of world developments through a free press and listening to the radio.

My education so far has been good. I had a sound religious education at the Franciscan seminary and then at a grammar school in Graz, where capable Austrian teachers taught. After Austria became part of Germany in 1938, the Nazis closed the seminary. At the time, I was seventeen years old. In 1939, when I was to be drafted into the army, I joined the Waffen SS (attending their medical academy in Graz) to start my medical studies. I continued my studies at the University of Graz until June 1944, when I was ordered to the front for the first time as a doctor. I rejected what they taught in the SS Military Academies and viewed my time spent there as wasted. I want my children taught in the pre-Nazi Austrian school system, with slightly more emphasis on physical training.'

Herwig, as you may have noticed, I have glossed over a few things here. I wasn't drafted into the army; I voluntarily joined the Waffen SS. I also omitted my first campaign in France in 1940. During my studies, I became broad-minded in my thinking and developed an ability to criticize my situation and understand some of society's problems. The narrow-minded style of Nazi education never impressed me.

I cannot shape my future now. Everything will depend on the conditions I find upon my return to Austria. I plan to finish my last year of studies in Graz or Vienna, specializing in psychology, and work in my father-in-law's hospital in St. Pölten near Vienna, which is now in the Russian occupation zone, provided this option is available to me. If Austria becomes a democratic country, I would like to contribute as much as possible to its democratic way of life. However, as long as Austria is under Russian control, I don't want to return. I certainly don't want to be forced to fight for Russia in the event of a new war, not even as a medic to save the lives of friends and foe alike.'

TRANSLATION SERVICE – FIRED

In January 1946, I was removed from the Translation Service and transferred to a POW camp in Wisconsin. Only now can I read the letter requesting my dismissal from the Translation Service. I was not asked any questions at the time, so I could not defend myself. Here is the letter:

```
SECRET                        January 31, 1946
Post Box 1142, Alexandria, Virginia
INTERNAL OFFICE MEMORANDUM/CIRCULAR
TO: Capt. Holbrook

SUBJECT: P/W's working as Trustees

After careful investigation of the
present Trustee Complement, it has been
found that two subjects at present working
in the Translation Section do not meet the
requirements and political standards
necessary to hold a position of trust.

Salmutter, Sepp, Obersturmführer (Ober-
leutnant). This man volunteered for the
Waffen SS in 1939, and his last unit was
the 1st Battalion SS Panzer Artillery
Regiment Das Reich. On December 16, 1944,
he participated in the Ardennes
Offensive and operated in the vicinity
of Gouvy-Medrin-Laroche. Prior to being
transferred to this front, P/W had oper-
ated in June 1944 on the invasion front
with the 2nd SS Panzer Division. This
division moved up from southwest France
and is known to have committed atrocities
in this area. The 2nd SS Panzer Division
```

POST OFFICE BOX 1142
ALEXANDRIA, VIRGINIA

POST OFFICE BOX 1142
ALEXANDRIA, VIRGINIA

31 January 1946

INTER-OFFICE MEMORANDUM

TO : Captain Holbrook

SUBJECT : P/W's working as trustees

1. After careful investigation of the present Trustee Complement it has been found that two subjects at present working in the Translation Section do not meet the requirements and political standards necessary to hold a position of trust.

2. SALMUTTER, Sepp, Obersturmfuehrer (Oberleutnant). This man volunteered for the Waffen SS in 1939 and his last unit was the 1st Battalion SS Panzer Artillery Regiment Das Reich. On 16 December 1944 he participated in the Ardennes offensive and operated in the vicinity of Gouvy-Cadrin-Laroche. Prior to being transferred to this front P/W had operated in June 1944 on the invasion front with the 2nd SS Panzer Division. This Division moved up from southwest France and is known to have committed atrocities in this area. The 2nd SS Panzer Division is also responsible for the massacre at Oradour.

3. Subject's background contains a series of Nazi indoctrinations: 1940, SS Aerztliche Akademie, Graz; 1941, SS Junkerschule, Toelz; 1941, SS NCO School, Lauenburg; 1942, SS Junkerschule Braunschweig; 1942-44, member of the SS Military Academy. As a "medical student" P/W visited concentration camps at Dachau, Oranienburg, and Buchenwald. Due to the nature of the secrecy in which these concentration camps were kept it seems very doubtful that anybody not regarded as an absolutely trustworthy disciple of Nazism would be permitted to enter these "sacred" Nazi institutions. On 2 April 1942 subject was classified "zum SS Fuehrer im Sanitaetsdienst geeignet" (suitable for appointment as SS Officer in the Medical Service).

4. The mere fact that P/W fought his way through the front lines and remained at Gouvy to await capture does not necessarily show any particular love for democracy but must be regarded as the most practical form of self-preservation. The explanation for his neo-democratic views might be found in the fact that in March 1945 a comrade of his, the Battalion doctor of the Feld Ersatz Battalion of the SS Division Das Reich, Oberjunker Dr. Fronius, who was brought to the P/W camp at Namur, told him that he was considered a deserter and that it is probable that he had been dishonorably discharged from the SS and condemned to death.

6. It may be pointed out that at the time of appointment as Trustees Captain Krempel, as Morale Officer, voiced his doubts as to the sincerity of these men but was overruled in the final acceptance by the higher echelon of this Installation.

7. Due to the above mentioned conclusions these two men will be removed from this Post as quickly as proper arrangements can be made.

HERMAN L. WALLE
Captain, Inf.

Office Correspondence: Sepp Salmutter's Removal from the Translation Service

is also responsible for the massacre at Oradour.

Subject's background contains a series of Nazi-indoctrinations. 1940, SS Aerztliche Academy, Graz; 1941, SS Junkerschule, Toelz; 1941, SS NCO School, Lauenburg; 1942, SS Junkerschule, Braunschweig; 1942-1944, member of the SS Military Academy. As a "medical student," P/W visited concentration camps at Dachau, Oranienburg, and Buchenwald. Due to the nature of the secrecy in which these concentration camps were kept, it seems very doubtful that anybody not regarded as an absolutely trustworthy disciple of Nazism would be permitted to enter these "sacred" Nazi institutions. On April 2, 1942, subject was classified "zum SS Fuehrer im Sanitaetsdienst geeignet" (suitable for appointment as SS Officer in the Medical Service).

The mere fact that the P/W fought his way through the front lines and remained at Gouvy to await capture does not necessarily show any particular love for democracy, but it must be regarded as the most practical form of self-preservation. The explanation for his neo-democratic views might be found in the fact that in March 1945, a comrade of his, the Battalion doctor of the Field Ersatz Battalion of the SS Division Das Reich, Oberjunker Dr. Fronius, who was brought to the P/W camp at Namur, told him that he was considered a deserter and that it is probable that he had been dishonorably discharged from the SS and condemned to death.

It may be pointed out that at the time of appointment as Trustees, Captain Krempel, as Morale Officer, voiced his doubts as to the sincerity of these men but was overruled in the final acceptance by the higher echelon of this Installation.

Due to the above-mentioned conclusions, these two men will be removed from the post as quickly as proper arrangements can be made.

Herman L. Halle,
Captain, Inf.

The letter above is vexing, written on my twenty-fifth birthday. My immediate removal from the Translation Service was explained, amongst other things, by the possibility that I'd taken part in the Oradour massacre. In 1944, the 2nd SS Panzer Division Das Reich committed war crimes in Tulle and Oradour in Southern France. However, only 150 Waffen SS men were engaged, out of the more than twelve thousand who served in our Division, and I had not been guilty in any possible way. Furthermore, the letter indicated that I had merely wished to preserve my life and had 'not necessarily demonstrated any special passion for democracy.' A third argument offered was that only an absolutely trustworthy disciple of Nazism would be permitted to enter the concentration camps, which were 'sacred Nazi institutions'. The Americans concluded that I must have been a blindly trusting National Socialist because I'd followed orders to visit three concentration camps – Dachau, Buchenwald, and Sachsenhausen.

This document invites contemplation. All three claims had been known for a year since I became a prisoner-of-war, so why this sudden and immediate transfer from Fort Hunt to Columbus, Wisconsin? One must find the explanation for this report somewhere else. Was there a new boss who wanted to prove he was a tough guy and build a reputation for himself? Political guidelines may have shifted. The German Wehrmacht surrendered eight months earlier. The Nuremberg war crimes trial had begun two months before this letter was written, bringing German atrocities in occupied Europe to the world's attention. Possibly this prompted the American military administration to re-examine the backgrounds of all its detainees, particularly those from the Waffen SS, and to remove them from positions of trust. I can make guesses; the exact reason for my dismissal will remain a mystery.

What would the next step of my confinement entail? There was no telling how long I would stay imprisoned or how I should behave to get through my prison sentence safely. Whatever happened, I'd have to keep a low profile.

PRISONER-OF-WAR CAMP, COLUMBUS

After firing me from the Translation Service, in early February 1946, the Americans transported me north from Fort Hunt to Camp Columbus in Wisconsin. The camp, located near Columbus, a small town of around 3,000 people, housed 500 prisoners. Because few American guards spoke our language, German officers supervised the inmates and kept order. They roused our guys, marched them to and from the canteen, and got them ready for work. The routine instilled in the detainees a sense of military discipline. Sports and hobbies were encouraged. The camp provided us with writing and painting materials, woodworking tools, and musical instruments, and we were permitted to communicate with our families in Germany and Austria.

I was in charge of the prisoners' medical care from 8 until 10 every morning, with the help of an assistant paramedic. For more complicated and rare medical procedures, I had to refer some of my sick comrades to the city hospital. Following morning surgery, I worked in a neighboring farm's cowshed with other comrades. The work was not too demanding, and I enjoyed doing it. It was nearly as pleasant as my job as a translator at Fort Hunt. It reminded me of my boyhood in Niederschöckl, where I'd helped to feed my grandmother's cows and clean out the shed.

A total of 425,000 German prisoners came to the United States, and the Americans interned them in 700 camps spread across 46 states. Apart from the barbed wire and watchtowers, the camps resembled military training facilities in the United States or Germany. There were 38 camps in Wisconsin, holding around 40,000 German POWs. At the time, ethnic German farmers made up one-third of Wisconsin's population, many of them first or second generation immigrants who still spoke German at home. Though America and Germany had fought a horrible war, as prisoners, we shared a common culture with the local German immigrants. We bonded in a way an average American citizen could not always understand. Because there was such a massive demand for farmhands in Wisconsin, the American administration moved many of the German POWs there, thus alleviating the agricultural labor crisis. My fellow prisoners and I looked forward to heading out to work in the fields. We received cash for our efforts, and it helped to break up the monotony of detention at the camp, giving us a purpose. Prisoners also worked in canneries, mills and other sectors, posing a slight security risk.

We were only allowed to move outside the camps in a restricted area. Black American guards noted with some resentment that German POWs could eat in restaurants and diners where they were not permitted to enter. Fraternization between American women and German inmates was tolerated, although illegal. The prisoners got along well with the locals, drinking in pubs and meeting local girls. The camp staged social gatherings and on occasion invited Americans, where some German prisoners met their future wives.

As former SS officers, we considered ourselves fortunate to have been caught by Americans rather than the Soviets. In America, we were astounded by the comfort of the

Main Street, Columbus, Wisconsin, USA 1946
Sepp Salmutter served here in a POW camp

Pullman trains taking us to the camps. As far as we could tell, the military conflict had not harmed the country's economy. I adored the endless expanses of the American countryside.

The Geneva Convention stipulated that we receive compensation for our labor and that officers should not have to work. A portion of our income went towards funding the POW program, while the remainder was given to us as pocket money to spend at the camp canteen or in the town of Columbus. Many of my comrades discovered their living conditions in captivity to be superior to those in bombed-out Germany or, in my case, Austria. During my detention in the Wisconsin camp, I never heard about anyone trying to flee.

The Young Men's Christian Association, or YMCA, printed books and provided bookbinding materials so that if they became frayed by frequent usage, we could repair them. The camp had subscriptions for American newspapers. A group of artists published a newspaper including poems, short tales, puzzles, and games, all written in German. The authorities understood that publishing magazines provided inmates with a creative outlet while helping to maintain morale.

However, some prisoners were still immersed in Nazi ideology. When obliged to attend roll call beneath the US flag, they ridiculed the guards and saluted with 'Sieg Heil.' They continued to celebrate Hitler's birthday and other celebrations despite the Americans prohibiting such behavior. Comrades who had served under Rommel in the North African desert and been imprisoned for an extended period, found the German loss and surrender difficult to accept.

These incorrigibles burned swastikas into the shells of live turtles they had picked up in the countryside; some of them may still be crawling around today. A small fanatical gang of Nazis inside several camps executed any German comrade suspected of being anti-Nazi, disguising this deed as an accident. This group was known as the 'ghosts,' hence my needing to keep quiet about how I had ended up in captivity.

I took part in a formal re-education program on democracy for the prisoners, organized by the US government. My entire existence was a series of brainwashing – first by the Franciscans, followed by the SS, and now by the Americans in Wisconsin. If you think about it, every person's brainwashing begins in childhood. You are taught how to behave, how to speak, and how to look at things according to your family's background. I remember my German teacher telling me to 'listen to everything, before making a decision even if it contradicts your point of view.' This I did on occasion, revising my perspective.

> 'The Western Allies would be wise to educate intelligent POWs in the theory and practice of democracy and place them in positions of authority upon their return to a democratic postwar Germany.' [questionnaire]

For the entire year of 1946, I was a POW held in the United States. Like most other prisoners, I had the time of my life, and we left the country of our captivity feeling optimistic about America. We had learned the English language and had several hundred dollars in our pockets. After our repatriation, thousands of former POWs immigrated to the United States, and thousands more returned for visits. I too would have liked to return to Columbus, but once I had gone back to Austria, my financial situation prohibited me from doing so.

BARBARA

As a camp doctor in Columbus, Wisconsin, every day, I reported to the American camp administration about the health of prisoners and, if required, requested admissions to the local hospital.

During one of these assignments, I met Barbara O'Keefe, who worked in the camp office. She was a freckled, thirty-year-old blonde of Irish and Scandinavian ancestry. One day she invited me to her house for dinner. She picked me up in her Jeep, and we drove to a pleasant residential neighborhood on the outskirts of town, where her white wood-paneled bungalow stood. Barbara prepared dinner and taught me proper American table manners. She demonstrated how to cut a bite-sized piece of steak, then put down the knife at the side, place the fork in the right hand, and eat while sliding the left hand under the table, then repeat. Barbara took great interest in teaching me such things and seemed anxious to turn me into a good Yank. She laughed frequently and loudly, which she had every right to do as she lived in the world's most prosperous country, had an excellent career, and was healthy and good-looking. She was a 2nd lieutenant, one level below me, divorced and without children.

Late in the evening, on the way back to camp, she surprised me by saying, 'The day after tomorrow, you can come over to my house again, and you'll fuck me.' After a slight pause, she burst out laughing. Was it a command, or was it a joke?

Residential home, Columbus, Wisconsin, USA, 1946.
Barbara lived in the immediate vicinity.

We showered before and after sex on the next visit. Barbara began inviting me over two or three times a week. In her sizeable kitchen, she preferred to serve canned food, although she could have prepared meals from scratch. She liked reading periodicals rather than novels, but watching television was her favorite pastime.

We knew our relationship would not continue forever but we made the most of it. I admired Barbara, who was straightforward,uncomplicated, fun-loving, deodorant-fresh, and experienced with a mind untroubled by deep thought. However, a spark was lacking, and simply making love would not have been enough to keep us together. Resi, with whom I had clicked on many levels, had spoilt me in that regard.

Barbara shaved her underarms and groomed her 'lady garden.' According to her, most American men are circum-cised, although, in Europe, it was mostly only Jews who underwent this procedure. This was quite a crucial issue during the Nazi era, of course. If you were not snipped, nobody could take you for a Jew, which could save you from being sent to a concentration camp.

On Sundays, Barbara attended the Lutheran church and was a member of the congregation. Unlike in Austria, churches of several denominations lined the roads in Columbus, each interpreting the Holy Bible differently. Barbara was amazed and delighted that I knew the Bible so well. Americans take their religion seriously. I never told her that I had left the church, as I am pretty sure she would not have become involved with a non-believer.

We corresponded long after my return to Austria, right until the early 1960s, and Barbara was the middle name I gave to my eldest daughter. My imprisonment in America eventually ended, and the Americans transferred me to a prison in France, closer to home and where I had to adjust to new circumstances. I knew France through the campaigns but was apprehensive about being sent there. It was unlikely I would fare as well as I had in America.

VITRY-LE-FRANCOIS CAMP, FRANCE, 1947

I suspect my release from American captivity resulted from the wish to send all prisoners back home by the end of 1948. In April 1948, the four victorious powers sealed it in the Moscow Agreement.

The conditions in the French camp were disgusting. While there, I assisted the camp doctor, who was happy to have an extra pair of helping hands. As a POW in America, I never saw people suffering from physical emaciation and weakness. There were numerous such cases here, though, and it didn't take long to find out why. The food supply in France was not as catastrophic as it had been immediately after the war, but deliveries were often erratic, and there were still real shortages. The French civil population was suffering hardships, too. One week, the camp would receive a truckload of cauliflowers, and for the coming days, cauliflower soup would be on the menu. The following week, it would be carrots, with a daily menu of carrot soup. The accommodation was uncomfortable for all the prisoners, many of whom were forced to do dangerous work such as searching for unexploded mines or working underground in coal mines. Most prisoners of war sent to this camp were worn out and incapable of any valuable work. Perhaps this had led to their early release from previous camps.

Unlike in America, the camp inmates had to stay within the campground. There was no camp newspaper, no music,

© Herwig Salmutter

Prisoner camp, 1947
Sepp Salmutter in France for the third time

and no theatre or board games. I had plenty of time to listen to various, sometimes harrowing, accounts from fellow prisoners about their war experiences, but I held back from disclosing my true past.

How relieved I was, after three months in this hell-hole, to receive my discharge papers! I couldn't wait to go home, but was unsure what to expect. You were four years old, Herwig. How would I find you and Gretl, and where?

HOMECOMING TO AUSTRIA, 1947

After my release from the prisoner-of-war camps, I searched for you and Gretl and soon found you in Niederschöckl.

Gretl had stayed in Graz until the fall of 1944, looking after you while living in a rented flat and studying. After the heavy bombing raids on Graz, she moved to be with my grandmother. In early November 1944, she fled from the approaching Russians to Gmunden in Upper Austria.

In the summer of 1945, after the war had ended and once the Russians had moved out of Styria into the province of Lower Austria, Gretl once again returned to the village of Niederschöckl to live with my relatives. Neither Gretl's father nor her stepmother, Gerti, wanted her to move in with them as reconciliation was out of the question. Though Gretl kept little contact with her father, he supported her during and after the war.

Before describing our life in the village, let me tell you what Austria looked like after losing the war: I hardly recognized my homeland. 'Adolf Hitler Square' had again become 'Main Square,' flags with swastikas had given way to red-white-red Austrian flags, and the province of 'Upper Danube' had once again become 'Upper Austria.' However, the war and its aftermath brought far more profound changes.

During the last days of the war, the provincial leader, Gauleiter Uiberreither, was still raging against the opponents of the Nazi regime. In Graz, political prisoners were shot without trial. The Nazis executed a captured Allied aircrew who had to bail out of their bomber in the last major air raid. During the last days of Nazi rule, Waffen SS fanatics shot German soldiers for desertion and civilians for doubting the final German victory.

Although the war's end brought euphoria at the liberation from the National Socialist regime of terror, the precarious food situation posed a significant problem. As mentioned earlier, people received little more than 800 kilo calories per day in the first months of peace time. These poor nutritional conditions led to an increase in infant and child mortality. Only foreign food aid helped Austria through the harsh winter of 1945/46; in 1946, sixty percent of food rations were still coming from overseas aid.

The four powers had restored the Austrian state to the borders existing in 1938 before the Anschluss. They divided the country into four occupation zones, controlled by the victorious powers: the USA, Britain, France, and Russia. The end of the war had not brought about stability. The Russians and the Americans discussed a peace conference, but in time the differences between the occupying powers grew ever more prominent.

On the one side, the Western Allies wanted to re-establish liberal democracies under the political and economic control of the USA. On the other side, the Soviet Union wanted to establish Moscow's influence over the largest possible territory. The Communist Party eliminated all

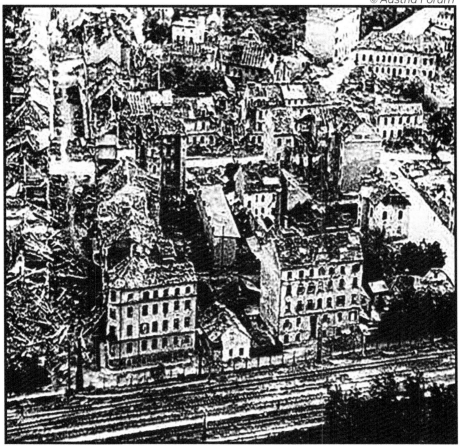

Bomb damage in the area of the Graz Central Station, 1945

opposition through terror and persecution. Millions of displaced German-speaking people fleeing the Eastern parts, whether complicit or not, paid dearly for the crimes of the National Socialists.

A new Austrian government began to form. In April 1945, Leopold Figl had been released from death row, having only escaped execution thanks to the sudden collapse of the Nazi regime. While in the concentration camp, he held talks with socialists and communists and sought common ground. Before the war, he had been a member of the Christian-Socialist Farmers' Union and was now trying to cooperate with his political opponents from the 1930s. Figl was one of the co-founders of the Conservative Austrian People's Party. He was a persuasive communicator and knew how to present a vision for a better future to the country's starving population.

During the long years of war, the role of women in society had changed. Many men had fallen; others had been absent for a long time due to war and captivity and only returned home years after the end of the war. Women had shouldered the responsibility, not only of raising children but also of ensuring the survival of their whole family. Many kids like you hardly knew their fathers. There were cases where those who had been declared fallen unexpectedly returned home, only to find their wives had remarried. After former soldiers reverted to their previous occupations, women went back to their prior domestic roles. Marriage and family were encouraged as the most desirable goals in women's lives, resulting in a baby boom.

DENAZIFICATION
AT GRAZ UNIVERSITY

At the time of my release from the prison camps, all my knowledge about post-war Austria had come from American publications. Back home, I was astounded at what had become of all the Nazis at the university and throughout my country.

Perhaps it would be fairer and more comprehensive if I wrote to you from today's perspective about how denazification happened firstly in the German occupation zones. In 1949, two German states were founded: East Germany (the German Democratic Republic) and West Germany (the Federal Republic of Germany).

In East Germany, the justice ministry handled criminal trials quickly and thoroughly. It rigorously denazified the judicial administration and replaced judges with new ones who supported socialism.

In West Germany, the whole judicial administration, including former judges operating during the Third Reich, were reintegrated, except for high-ranking Nazi functionaries or those proven to have participated in Nazi crimes.

Both German states treated professionals and technical specialists necessary for the reconstruction or research with more clemency.

In Austria, people had changed their political convictions overnight and declared themselves to have always been enemies of National Socialism. Austrians pretended to have been the first victims of the enforced integration into the German Reich. The Allied occupying powers – in Styria, the British – implemented denazification only half-heartedly and released Austrian Nazis after the briefest detention. Decision-making in those proceedings was complicated because most former National Socialists managed to get a respectable Democrat to vouching for them. Let me describe the circumstances of three of my favorite professors at the end of the war:

Prof. Dr. Hans Lieb: Once the war was over, his previous lectures on the chemistry of warfare agents landed him in trouble. His recognized scientific competence protected him from political prosecution, and he soon returned to teaching at the university. In November 1949, as provost, he signed my medical degree.

Prof. Dr. Anton Hafferl: As mentioned earlier, he was the administrator of the Nazi Lecturers' Association, a friend of the Styrian Gauleiter, Siegfried Uiberreither, and a friend of the head of my SS Medical Academy, SS Sturmbannführer Bernward Gottlieb. The corpses he provided for his students' practical anatomy studies were those of executed freedom fighters and other victims of the Gestapo, the secret Nazi police force. After the war, the British military occupation authorities imprisoned Prof. Hafferl for his Nazi affiliations. Still, after a short investigation, they permitted him to continue teaching his students in the Anatomy department for another ten years until he retired.

Prof. Dr. Alfred Pischinger: He had been an illegal Nazi party member before 1934, and from 1938, a member of the SA Storm Troopers. As a distinguished expert, he supported the so-called doctrine of Racial Hygiene and acted as a judge at the Graz Higher Court of Hereditary Health. His research specialized in histo-chemistry and he became part of a scientific network at the University of Graz from 1939 to 1945, experimenting on pregnant women and their fetuses

In 1945, when the university dismissed Dr. Alfred Pischinger without prior notice, eight medical students, two of whom claimed to have been members of an Austrian anti-Nazi resistance movement, called for his reinstatement, proclaiming that he had not taught Nazi theories in his Genetics course. Stretching incredibility further, they declared that Dr. Alfred Pischinger had resisted pressure from the provincial Nazi leader to give preferential treatment in the university examinations to students from the SS Medical Academy.

Dr. Pischinger continued his academic career unhindered, despite his Nazi activities. Since 1958, and to this day, he has been head of the Histological Embryological Institute at the University of Vienna. He has also become famous for his work on scientific alternatives and holistic approaches to medicine. His past and his fetal experiments seem to have disappeared from public knowledge.

Most of the professors who taught me during the Nazi dictatorship had close links to the Nazi movement. They were heads of academic Nazi institutions, members of the Nazi party, and taught Race Theories. I am convinced

Grazer Blutgericht vollzog 155 Todesurteile

Freiheitskämpfer wurden seziert — Die Affäre Hafferl

G r a z, 16. September (ACA). Oberlandesgerichtspräsident Dr. Z i g e u n e r übergab jetzt der Presse Tatsachenmaterial über die Zahl der während der nationalsozialistischen Herrschaft in G r a z verhängten, beziehungsweise vollstreckten T o d e s u r t e i l e. Den Anlaß zu dieser Veröffentlichung bietet das Erscheinen des angekündigten österreichischen „Rotbuches" und die Behandlung der Angelegenheit des Univ.-Prof. H a f f e r l in den Zeitungen.

Gegen Prof. H a f f e r l, den Leiter des Anatomischen Instituts der Universität Graz, wurde vor einiger Zeit die Beschuldigung erhoben, daß er noch nach dem Zusammenbruch der deutschen Herrschaft in Österreich mehrere Leichen hingerichteter F r e i h e i t s k ä m p f e r aus dem Institut in aller Heimlichkeit hatte abtransportieren und menschenunwürdig v e r s c h a r r e n lassen, anstatt sofort den Behörden über das Vorhandensein dieser Überreste von Opfern der nationalsozialistischen Blutjustiz Meldung zu machen und so zur Klärung vieler Fälle beizutragen. Im Laufe der Untersuchung der Sache war Prof. H a f f e r l seines Postens e n t h o b e n worden.

Namen der Toten geheimgehalten

Die Akten aus der Zeit der nationalsozialistischen Besetzung wurden vor dem Zusammenbruch leider teilweise vernichtet. Eine genaue Überprüfung des noch geretteten Aktenmaterials ergab, daß an der in G r a z eigens geschaffenen, raffiniert ausgestatteten Hinrichtungsstätte, die am 2. August 1943 „in Betrieb" gesetzt wurde, bis zum 13. März 1945, also in etwas mehr als anderthalb Jahren, 155 T o d e s u r t e i l e vollstreckt wurden. Weiter wurden 147 Urteile an anderen Exekutionsstätten (Feliferhof, SS-Kaserne, Gestapo Wien) ausgeführt. Dem A n a t o m i s c h e n I n s t i t u t der Universität Graz wurden 89 Leichen übergeben, also bei weitem nicht der gesamte „Anfall". Nach dem Oktober 1944 nahm die Universität keine weiteren mehr an. Die N a m e n wurden nach Möglichkeit g e h e i m g e h a l t e n, nur wenige Leichname von dem Staatsanwalt den Angehörigen der Opfer zur Bestattung freigegeben.

Die S c h e u Prof. Dr. Hafferls, justizierte Personen sezieren zu lassen, erklärt die verhältnismäßig große Zahl der bei der Befreiung im Institut vorhandenen Leichen Hingerichteter. Unter 44 Leichen befanden sich die der hier namentlich angeführten:

Andreas D r e x l e r, Johann S t r a ß e r, Franz S t r o h m a y e r, Johann S t e l z e r, Lorenz P o k e t z, Helene S e r v e c z, Eduard P e t l, Johann S e r k e s c h, Iwan Z i w i r k i. Die Aufzeichnungen fielen auch hier den Kriegseinwirkungen vielfach zum Opfer.

Christliche Bestattung nach Kriegsende

Aus den polizeilichen Erhebungen in der Sache Hafferl führt Oberlandesgerichtspräsident Dr. Z i g e u n e r folgendes an:

Dr. H a f f e r l behauptet, kaum widerlegbar, schon im Mai 1945 dem Sicherheitsdirektor vom Vorhandensein der 44 Leichen M i t t e i l u n g g e m a c h t zu haben. Er habe eine Weisung abwarten wollen.

Die Tatsache der Überführung von Leichen Justifizierter in die Anatomie ist verbürgt und auch dem Kommando der Roten Armee bekanntgeworden. Dr. Hafferl traf Vorbereitungen, die Leichen zum Abtransport gesondert bereitzustellen. Als die Weisung der Sicherheitsdirektion ausblieb, sprach er bei Landeshauptmannstellvertreter M a c h o l d, dem Chef des steirischen Gesundheitswesens, vor, und veranlaßte die Beerdigung durch die Bestattungsanstalt.

Die Leichen wurden am Tage in der Anatomie abgeholt, auf den Zentralfriedhof übergeführt, dort e i n g e s e g n e t und am T a g e beerdigt.

Ein Tatbestand nach dem Kriegsverbrechergesetz ist daher nicht gegeben, weshalb gegen Dr. Hafferl auch k e i n V o r f a h r e n in der Angelegenheit eingeleitet wurde.

Über Wunsch des KZ-Verbandes werden ab 16. d. M. Häftlinge beigestellt, um für eine w ü r d i g e B e g r ä b n i s s t ä t t e der Justifizierten zu sorgen.

Graz Blood Court carried out 155 death sentences

Freedom fighters were dissected - The Hafferl Scandal

GRAZ. 16 September 1945 (ACA). The President of the Higher Regional Court, Dr. Zigeuner, now handed over to the press factual material on the number of death sentences passed or executed in Graz during the National Socialist regime. The reason for this publication is the announcement of the forthcoming Austrian "Red Book" in which Prof. Hafferl will be investigated by the newspapers.

Prof. Hafferl, director of the Anatomical Institute of the University of Graz, some time ago was accused of having had several corpses of executed freedom fighters secretly transported from the Institute and buried inhumanely after the collapse of German rule in Austria. Instead he should have reported immediately the existence of the remains of these National Socialist victims of 'blood justice' to the authorities and thus would have contributed to the clarification of many cases. During the course of this investigation, Prof. Hafferl was removed from his post.

Names of the dead kept secret

Unfortunately, the files from the time of the National Socialist occupation were partially destroyed before the collapse. A close examination of the still-salvaged file material revealed that 155 death sentences had been carried out at the specially created, ingeniously equipped place of execution in Graz, which began operating on 2 August 1943 until 13 March 1945, lasting just over one and a half years. Altogether 155 death sentences were executed.

Furthermore, 147 death sentences were carried out at other execution sites (Feliferhof, SS barracks, Vienna Gestapo). 89 corpses were handed over to the Anatomical Institute of the University of Graz, although many more were available; then from October 1944, the university no longer had use for any more corpses. As far as was possible the names of the victims were kept secret. Only a few of the victims' bodies were handed back to relatives by the public prosecutor for burial.

The relatively large number of executed corpses that were held at the Institute at the time of Austria's liberation can be explained by Prof. Dr. Hafferl's said reluctance to have executed persons dissected. Out of 44 corpses only the following can be named:

Andreas Drexler, Johann Straßer, Franz Strohmayer. Johann Stelzer, Lorenz Poketz, Helene Servecz, Eduard Petl, Johann Serkesch, Iwan Zwirkl. Here too records were lost because of the war.

Christian burial after the end of the war

Based on the police investigations in the Hafferl case the Higher Regional Court President Dr. Zigeuner states the following:

Dr. Hafferl's claim to have informed the Security Director as early as May 1945 about the existence of the 44 corpses can't be refuted. He then had been waiting for instructions.

The Red Army Head Quarters confirm that they had knowledge of the fact that executed corpses had been transferred to the university's anatomy department. Dr. Hafferl had prepared the bodies for taking away from there. When the Security Directorate failed to give instructions about what should be done with the corpses, Dr. Hafferl approached the head of the Styrian health service, Vice President of the Provincial Administration, Mr. Machold and then arranged for funerals to be carried out by a funeral home.

The bodies were collected from the Anatomy Department during office hours, transferred to the central cemetery where they were duly blessed and buried during daylight hours.

Therefore, no offence under the War Crimes Act had been committed, which is why no proceedings were initiated against Dr. Hafferl in this matter.

At the request of the Concentration Camp Association, starting from the 16th of this month, detainees will be made available to ensure dignified burials for the executed corpses take place.

Professor Dr. Hafferl let his students dissect Gestapo victims the professors' disastrous political and moral influence upon their young and devoted students had catastrophic consequences. We followed them blindly. In my opinion, the British occupation forces carried out the denazification process far too leniently. Either they were not in full command of the German language, or they placed too much value on the word of educated Austrians, who put university professors on pedestals.

The new government adhered to the system of giving amnesty to all collaborators and persons who had been 'led astray,' especially the young. However, they removed so-called 'illegals' (those who had been Nazi party members before the Anschluss) and ex-Nazi administrators from their posts. The "Austrian National Socialist Registration Decree" of June 1945 read:

> 'Whoever can prove that he never took advantage of his affiliation with the NSDAP or the SS... and who can demonstrate by his conduct before the liberation of Austria that he had a positive attitude toward the independent Republic of Austria, may submit a request for leniency.'

The Graz University Rector opposed the administration of the city of Graz for conscripting ex-Nazi members to clean up all rubble left by the Allied bombings. These included professors, lecturers, assistants, civil servants, and employees of the university who were required to register as ex-Nazis. The Rector submitted to the City's Labor Office an extensive list of university staff who, in his opinion, could not be spared from their duties. He wanted them exempted from forced manual labor, and the Labor Office complied with his wishes.

It appeared that no one had been guilty; it was a case of gullible people being seduced and led astray. At least, that is how the denazification process in Austria seemed to me, but I cannot deny that this tolerant attitude also worked to my benefit!

Whitewashing the past, the Steirerblatt newspaper of January 24, 1946, wrote a glowing article about a new student generation to which I, too, belonged:

> 'Many students have had to see their youthful idealism turned in the wrong direction by the events of the last few years. Hardship and deprivation, the deaths of so many comrades, and disapointment have become the constant companion of their lives. Illusions have been shattered, plans for the future have dried up, and trust has been met by betrayal. However, to the credit of all our students, it can be said that most of them turned away from Nazi ideals. It is not evident that they had ever been Nazi followers.'

The communist newspaper Die Wahrheit of February 10, 1946, railed against this viewpoint:

> 'Is this ignorance or an effort to cover up all that has been? It seems to have been forgotten that Graz's students set fire to the Jewish temple in 1939, desecrated the Jewish synagogue, and took part in pogroms. Let us remember how, in 1938, in the lecture halls, upon the arrest of our Graz Jewish Nobel Prize winners Hess and Loewy, the academic youth, almost without exception and full of hate, chanted 'Saujuden' (Jewish pigs).'

Mr. Hands, the British military government commissioner for education in Styria, wrote a critical article in the newspaper Die Wahrheit on February 16, 1946:

> 'Concerning the question of the Styrian University: After the Anschluss, Graz was awarded the title 'City of Popular Uprising'

for being the city contributing most to the spread of the Nazi movement in Austria. The University of Graz was a leader in spreading National Socialist ideas.'

In a detailed article, again in the communist Die Wahrheit, of March 6, 1946, and barely a year after the collapse of the Nazi regime, the Rector of the University of Graz, Prof. Dr. K. Rauch, asked for leniency for former collaborators and Party members:

'Anyone who thought he could sneak back into the university by giving false information will lose all sympathy, while students who were not true Nazi sympathizers, who honestly regret their Nazi participation, and who accept the new political spirit are welcome. Would it not be better to invite back reformed students who erred in the past instead of expelling them? Might they otherwise not create a dangerous body of hopeless desperadoes?

This brings me to the professors and lecturers. Here, too, our purge had been criticized as too half-hearted. However, the medical faculty alone has dismissed 29 out of 57 professors and lecturers, while the philosophy faculty has removed 51 out of 98. Out of 175 professors and lecturers, 92 have not been retained. What this means for a university should be clear to anyone who knows how difficult it is to find qualified replacements.

Now to the main question: Were the Graz University professors enthusiastic party members? Some yes, others undoubtedly not. I think the majority were not. National Socialism disrupted the academic work of many professors, some of whom took refuge in the protective [Nazi] Party, merely to shelter from a devastating hurricane threatening to uproot them; they became Party members without giving due consideration to the consequences. That is why there are so many collaborators among the professors alongside active Party members.'

How did I view the Nazi ideology in my innermost soul? Why had I not listened to Resi's advice? Was my desire to study medicine so irresistible that I had shied away from critical moral questions, or did I just put them out of my mind? Had I not been against Nazi ideology myself, yet closed my eyes to what I didn't want to see?

I wanted to escape the rural environment of my childhood, and in doing so, I told myself life would turn out fine. I believed becoming a doctor would be a good thing. How could I have foreseen that the war started by the National Socialists would cause millions of deaths? I wasn't a Nazi and did not join the Nazi party, but through my actions, whether consciously or not, I must admit with regret that I supported the Nazis, a small cog of no great importance, but millions of cogs like me had assisted similarly in the successful running of this regime.

In February 1947, the government issued a three-party agreement to introduce the 'National-Socialist Party Member Act,' classifying registered Nazis into three groups: war criminals, incriminated, and lesser-incriminated persons. In 1948, the Austrian government granted amnesty to half a million Lesser-Incriminated Nazis, who once again became eligible to vote. I benefited from this amnesty, ensuring that my Waffen SS past would not stand in the way of my future professional career.

After the war, unrepentant veterans of the Waffen SS joined to form a legal support association. For my part, I avoided all contact with veterans who still glorified their war actions. I would have loathed any celebration of my involvement in the unjust and brutal occupation of foreign lands.

I was relieved to have been denazified without a lengthy process and allowed to continue my career, first as a student and later as a doctor.

NIEDERSCHÖCKL AFTER 1947

Living in Niederschöckl was hard, especially for Gretl. Within the span of a few years, she had gone from a comfortable middle-class home with her parents to a rented flat in Graz and finally to a room in a dilapidated farmhouse. The entire village was still without electricity and tap water; nothing had changed since my childhood. Gretl had difficulty understanding the local dialect and barely communicated with the villagers. Niederschöckl was in abject poverty and had been left behind. She had to carry water from a hand-operated pump in the courtyard up to the flat on the first floor. There was not a single shop or coffee house and no meeting place where she could make friends. She needed to learn how to cook, dry mushrooms, and preserve jam and fruit compotes to store for the winter months.

You surely remember the first eleven years of your life in the small village. Your childhood and mine ended up being quite similar, marked by hardship, but happy. We both knew nothing else. At home, we conversed in standard German, whereas outside, you and all the other children spoke in the Styrian dialect.

There were three rooms rented-out in my grandmother's house. Since she had disapproved of my leaving the church and joining the Waffen SS, she gave us the smallest room under the roof with a window facing north. At least we got it rent-free. Dusty old wooden boards covered the floor. Later on, after the birth of more children, we needed more space, and I converted and insulated more of the attic.

Gretl, Herwig and Sepp Salmutter, Niederschöckl, 1947

When you were five years old, a paraffin lamp provided light in the evenings until we got electricity in 1948. Along with other village community members, I helped to dig holes for the power masts.

During the summer months, we went out into the forest early on Sunday mornings to pick mushrooms, just as I had done with Alois twenty years earlier.

The putrid farm animal slurry ran down both sides of the village road and smelled in the old farmhouse. The memory is probably tickling your nose even now as you read this! Do you remember me slaughtering chickens and rabbits and dissecting them with a surgeon's scalpel? You looked on and listened as I explained the function of each internal organ.

Several times a year, Barbara dispatched a parcel from America containing corned beef, spices, popcorn, and marshmallows; the latter two were still virtually unknown in Austria. In addition, she sent clothes and underwear, half of which I sold in the village to help our family through the bad times after the war.

During the 1951 federal presidential election, I put up posters in the village for Burghart Breitner. He had been a surgeon at the University of Innsbruck, was recognized for his professional qualifications, and had been a German nationalist. Though he had lived in Austria, he had joined the Nazi Party early on. In 1934, after the Austrian government banned the National Socialists, he resigned from the Party, but in 1939, he re-joined the NSDAP. Once he had been successfully denazified, the 'Association of Independents' nominated Breitner as a non-party candidate, but he lost the election to Theodor Körner.

'Salmutter does not want to join any political organization after the war.' [eavesdropped]

I attended socialist and communist assemblies but joined neither Party. At a book reading by the Soviet author Mikhail Sholokhov, organized by the communists, he handed me a signed copy of his novel The Silent Don.

As a student until 1949, and then as a young doctor, I earned very little. By the time you were ten years old, I had five children and wanted a way out of this wretched misery. In 1949, when I obtained my doctorate in medicine, both you and Gretl were at the university's presentation. In the early days of practicing as a doctor, I cycled daily to work in Graz, but later on, I bought myself a motorbike. On night duties several times a week, I slept at the hospital where I specialized in trauma surgery under Professor Böhler, the 'father of trauma surgery.'

By the way, the word 'surgeon' comes from the Greek 'χειροργία' via the Latin 'chirurgia' and means manual labor or handicraft, and that is what I appreciate about my profession. It is practical work, requiring dexterity and experience whilst being based on theoretical knowledge. Though I have to wear orthopedic soles in my shoes for the long strenuous hours standing on my feet, I still love my job.

I delivered my fifth child Susi in 1953, in what proved to be a difficult home birth. When born, she was dark blue and had to be dipped alternately into hot and cold buckets of water. In the report I completed later, I was listed as father, doctor and midwife all rolled into one. How I love a challenge!

GERMAN DEMOCRATIC REPUBLIC

According to the Christian faith, the Romans nailed Jesus Christ, aged thirty-three, to the cross. What had he accomplished in his life, what had he seen, how had he helped, how could he look back on his short life? And how did I compare? What had I achieved? What were my plans for the future? While not becoming despondent, I was not satisfied with my professional career. Although I'd come back from the war in one piece, the present state of affairs was not to my liking.

In 1954, thirty-three years of age, I lived in an attic flat in an old farmhouse, without running water and no indoor toilet. Hospital doctors in Graz were poorly paid – not what I had hoped or studied so hard for.

The previous year, I'd decided that we would emigrate to build a better life abroad. The Nazi regime had exempted medical students from military service during the war. This anomaly had created a surplus of doctors in Austria, while there was an immense shortage of medics elsewhere in the world. As an unmarried doctor, I could have practiced in many countries without thinking twice. But as a father of five children, I had to consider local diseases, standards of schools and the language spoken before making a final decision.

In the end, I had to turn down an offer to move to Indonesia, as it was a difficult assignment to take on with young children. South-west Africa, where many people spoke German, would have been better. A friendly older gentleman at the consulate, expressing himself in perfect German, told me that the African climate was pleasant and healthy. He described a fascinating landscape of mountains, gorges, dunes, the sea and a wilderness with lions, giraffes, zebras, and where Hottentots* lived on the savanna.

* expression in use in 1969

The GDR, the German Democratic Republic, also recruited doctors. They offered a health service comparable to European standards and good schools. Speaking German, we would fit in easily. However, I had to consider the political situation. The world was then living in the darkest days of the Cold War, and its hottest zone lay between East and West Germany, both ideologically and militarily. The catastrophic Second World War had ended nine years ago, and the first signs of the West German economic miracle were beginning to show; it was a time of hope, and living standards were rising. At the same time, humanity was under the constant threat of nuclear annihilation, with both East and West demonizing one another. The very word 'communism' terrified us.

Nevertheless, after weighing all the pros and cons, I decided that Africa was too far, and we should instead emigrate to the GDR. As I had done before in my life, I wrestled with the old problem: getting something I wished for, at the price of being involved with a dictatorship. This time, the regime's goal was to build socialism in East Germany, and the government called itself, unapologetically, a 'Workers and Peasants dictatorship.' To get some more factual information about life and employment possibilities in East Germany, I boarded the Vindobona express train from Vienna to East Berlin, and presented myself at the Ministry of Health.

Upon my arrival, an official drove me from East Berlin's central railway station to the guest house belonging to the Ministry. Berlin still showed the devastating signs of war, including decaying ruins amongst new socialist buildings like the Stalin Allee Boulevard. On June 17 the previous year, the police had put down a revolt against the communist regime. My interviewer was aware I knew of this, and it formed the basis of our conversation. I had something to contribute to the GDR, and they had something to offer me. Moreover, for the GDR to hire a doctor from the West was a political coup, as most doctors moved from East to West.

Dr. Loch, a distinguished elderly physician and fortunately not someone from the bureaucratic administration, interviewed me. He was relaxed and spoke more openly than I had expected, politely inquiring about my trip, the accommodation and the food before getting straight to the point.

> 'Dr. Salmutter, we would like you to look around and check out our young republic. I would like to make you what we believe to be a fair offer. If you agree in principle, we will drive you to the town of Waren in Mecklenburg, where you can discuss your job prospects with your prospective boss. Back in Berlin, I will be at your disposal to answer any further questions you may have, and, providing everything works out, we could then sign the employment contract.'

Dr. Loch had my handwritten curriculum vitae in front of him. He had studied it well enough not to have to leaf through it during the job interview. In the application, I had declared my military service as having been with the Wehrmacht and not the Waffen SS, but I believe he knew the truth.

'You know, Mr. Salmutter, what's past is past. Evil people had misled many of us, and especially younger men like you. We are building a socialist country; few of our people had been communists. What counts for us today is the present, how people think and behave.

The health system in the GDR is non-political; most doctors have neither time nor interest in pursuing politics. I would advise you to remain a foreigner, focus on your job, and keep out of affairs of the state. Opponents of our young socialist state will try to get you onto their side. Please heed my advice and don't get involved. This way, both your professional and private life will be a success and to our mutual benefit.

After your stay in the USA and your education in Austria, the GDR might seem petit-bourgeois to you. I assure you – and we count on your cooperation – we will build a health system that is the envy of the world. I, too, occasionally have doubts about our political leaders and their actions, but allow me once more to stress the fact that health care is above politics, and only qualified doctors will decide upon our young country's health service.'

That sounded encouraging, and Dr. Loch presented details of the job offer. I would sign an exclusive contract giving me a long list of advantages over and above the standard employment document. My pay and promotion prospects would be excellent, my children would go to the best schools, and the state would guarantee their university admission. After dinner, Dr. Loch excused himself, explaining that he had to go back to the Charité hospital where he worked as an internist. I liked what I heard and, in principle, agreed to the offer.

The following day, they drove me to Mecklenburg in one of those Russian stretch limousines fashionable in the mid-1950s. Regularly spaced trees lined the asphalted country roads, and the flat countryside and lakes reminded me of the three months' training I had gone through in 1941 in Lauenburg, further to the east and now belonging to Poland.

My future boss was friendly and showed me around the hospital. They were in urgent need of a trauma surgeon. He told me that I could work overtime and take on more than one post. I expressed my enthusiasm for the offer and promised to think about it. Also, Dr. Loch's warning came true: one young doctor pulled me aside and cautioned me, saying it would be better for me to remain in Austria. In the afternoon, I strolled along the lakeshore, enjoying the view of bathers relaxing or playing ball games on the crowded sandy beach and of sailing boats in the distance.

Next day, back in East Berlin, Dr. Loch and I signed the employment contract. He told me that I would not be the only doctor to come from Austria to the GDR.

I resigned from my job in Graz and took a fortnight's holiday in Niederschöckl to prepare for the move.

Sepp Salmutter, MD, East Germany, 1958

The whole country was going crazy over the ongoing Football World Cup won by the Germans – to be specific, by the West Germans. We were waiting for the furniture van to arrive from the GDR. We wouldn't be taking many goods with us, only an attractive wooden inlaid table, my books, clothes, and bedding. I had sold my motorbike and given all that remained to my uncle. Once we had packed the goods and the van was on its way, we took the train to East Germany.

I looked with optimism to a future with improved living conditions and expected our family life to flourish. In the GDR, we would still remain Austrian citizens. Whatever happened, they couldn't do anything to us. For holidays in 'capitalist foreign countries,' as Dr. Loch had referred to them, we would only be able to exchange a small amount of Western currency. Still, we would be able to travel without hindrance whenever we wanted. Food stamps were still required in the GDR, but the shops were full of life's necessities. Some shortages were still to be expected, as only nine years had passed since the end of the war.

The Niederschöckl misery had come to an end. As a surgeon, I would perform far more operations than I ever could in Graz. I benefited from the shortage of doctors in East Germany; no one would interfere with an experienced trauma surgeon. I was not a sociable companion, but I was a qualified specialist, and that's how it would remain. Life was improving, but still, I wondered – would there be a price to pay at some point?

FEDERAL REPUBLIC OF GERMANY

I practiced for ten years in the GDR, first in Mecklenburg and then in Leipzig, followed by five years in Dresden and East Berlin. All in all, I did not regret having moved to the GDR. However, in 1961, halfway through my stint, the working conditions became more difficult. The hospital administration asked me to provide annual political assessments of my subordinates, and there it was – the price I'd feared I would have to pay. But I refused to spy on my colleagues. As an Austrian citizen in a secure and privileged position, I knew I did not have to bow to the dictate of communist administrators.

I continued to enjoy my work, but life in the country was no longer progressing as I had anticipated. Increasingly, I suspected that the regime had its people under constant surveillance. Since the building of the Berlin Wall in 1961, the communist government had complete control over its population. The GDR was supposed to prosper, with better living conditions under a controlled dictatorship, rather than under the random freedom of the West, but there was an everwidening gap between the living standards of East and West. I was still young enough to work elsewhere for another twenty years. Having performed more surgical operations in the GDR than my peers in West Germany, it would not be difficult for me to find a top job on the other side of the border.

In 1964, we moved from East to West Germany, or to give its official name, the Federal Republic of Germany.

First, we went to Mannheim for a year, then after a short stint in Weingarten to Ravensburg, where I worked again as a trauma surgeon. We remained Austrian citizens.

In Ravensburg, in the province of Württemberg, I practiced in a modern regional hospital. I lived with Gretl and the six children in a rented garden flat. Three years earlier, you had left to study in Austria. Your siblings were used to changing schools and managed to adapt to the school curriculum in the West. Meanwhile, I bought a big second-hand Mercedes and Volkswagen shares. Now that's what I call assimilation!

In the summer of 1965, I came to Leoben to see you graduate from the Mining University with a degree in Petroleum Engineering. Sixteen years earlier, you had been to my graduation, and now it was my turn to go to yours. I slept in Uncle Karl's garden house, not far from the town center. Karl, now a pensioner, had remained an unreformed Nazi. In the evening, we celebrated your success in a pub on the main square.

Herwig and Sepp Salmutter
at Herwig's graduation as Petroleum Engineer
at the Mining University in Leoben, Austria, 1965

HOSPITAL SHIP MS HELGOLAND

Slowly, Herwig, my story is coming full circle. I stayed in Ravensburg for four years. Two years ago, I bought a bungalow in St. Radegund near Graz, and my family moved there in the summer of 1968. I planned to stay one more year in Germany before joining them.

As I didn't feel ready to move back to Austria, I kept looking around for more exciting employment and eventually I came across a job offer with the German Red Cross in South Vietnam. The working conditions seemed attractive, and I quickly accepted. I provided full support for my family in our new home, so I knew I could leave without undue worry. In any case, the position needed filling urgently, so there was no time for discussions with the family.

My decision to go to Vietnam must have surprised you too. After many years of a conventional life, it was time for me to turn things in another direction. I felt that I was still too young to live out a run-of-the-mill existence in a provincial hospital. When the Red Cross accepted my application, I felt like I'd won the lottery. The war wouldn't bother me. For me, the decisive factor was not who was fighting whom but the chance to see the world and at the same time help people in need. I intend to work here for a few years, with half-yearly holidays back to Austria. Ideal for all, I would say.

I have been living in South Vietnam for four months now. War is raging through the country. Here in the city of Da Nang, the fighting is not too intense. Upon my arrival,

I received a warm welcome from my colleagues on the German Red Cross ship, the MS Helgoland. They are happy to have one more surgeon to tackle the massive load. We bring injured people on board, and there are always long queues awaiting treatment. The South Vietnamese Foreign Ministry has contractually agreed on the terms of the ship's deployment – the Fourth Geneva Convention protects the mission of the ship. We are only allowed to treat civilians, never American or Vietnamese war combatants.

The first impressions of Vietnam knocked me out. Before my arrival, my knowledge of this country came from TV news, magazines, and a coffee table book I had bought specifically to prepare me for the trip. Being in the heat and noise of an Asian city, amidst the many public outdoor eateries exuding aromas of unfamiliar spices, is something I will never forget.

Allow me to describe my new place and satisfy your interest in technology and numbers. The ship is 91 meters long and 14 meters wide, with a draft of over 4 meters; at 6000 hp, it can do a good 21 knots per hour – so our mechanic told me yesterday. Everything here is spotlessly clean and organized with German thoroughness. The Helgoland is equipped as a hospital ship and has 150 beds for in-patient care. There are three operating theatres and four specialist departments (surgery, internal medicine, gynecology, and radiology). The outpatient ward is overcrowded, and we can't admit everyone. Medical care for the civilian population in this country is poor; most people live in poverty and are unable to afford basic medical treatment. The German Red Cross treats people free of charge.

Around 30 crew members are on duty, plus eight doctors and roughly 20 mainly young nurses. The time spent here will be exhausting but rewarding. My cabin is small, but it's mine, and it's lockable.

My shift starts in one hour. Before that, I am to meet a Vietnamese teacher who can teach me the local language. If I like her, I will soon start my first lesson...

... Finally, I can pause for breath. The shifts are long, and we see many distressing cases that shock even the most experienced medical professionals. Sometimes I am confronted with injuries that, as a trauma surgeon, I never encountered back in France and Belgium during the war. We often see people on the operating table burned by napalm. It is a substance that sticks to its targets and is practically impossible to put out. Terrible. As far as I can remember, the Americans dropped napalm bombs on their enemies from 1943 onward. Now, they are doing it here in Vietnam.

Although I specialize in treating patients with accident and war injuries, I also take care of people with worm infestations, bone fractures, open wounds, tuberculosis, and diseases of the respiratory organs. As a surgeon, I have to deal with whatever comes up. We work close to our limits, which is a good thing as it gives us less time to think about the horrors of war. But I don't want to complain. A few colleagues are on their second tour and are still coping well.

Knowing you, you will have already located Da Nang on the map and noticed that this city of 350,000 inhabitants lies in South Vietnam, situated in the center of the country, which makes it strategically important to the Americans.

**Medical ship 'Helgoland'
operated by the German Red Cross, South Vietnam, 1969**

Postcard Sepp Salmutter sent to his son Herwig:

Dear Herwig,   Da Nang, 9/28/1969
I've been here for almost a month now. I'm fine, the
climate suits me well. The work is very interesting and
varied. On the day of my arrival, the Viet Cong 'greeted'
me with a major attack on Da Nang, but for an old
soldier, it was nothing exciting. Let me hear from you!
Dr. S. Salmutter, GERMAN RED CROSS Hospital Ship
Helgoland, FPO 96695, San Francisco, USA

They built an airbase and naval port for their massive logistic operation. The war is constantly present and recently a missile struck nearby but, so far, the Viet Cong hasn't attacked the Helgoland. The entire crew is aware of the risk of becoming casualties. An imposing Red Cross marks the ship with the protective symbol, and we wear Red Cross uniforms both on duty and when strolling through town. Both the Americans and the North Vietnamese respect our humanitarian mission, affording us some measure of safety.

The battles between the so-called Vietcong and the US Forces occur at night. We leave the harbor late in the evening to avoid getting caught in the crossfire, returning at first light. To restock on goods from a German supply ship, the Helgoland must lift anchor to enter international waters further out at sea, because the supply ship is not insured to dock in a port within a war zone.

There are coffins on the upper deck, should something happen to us. I try not to dwell on such thoughts, but it is hard not to consider the possibility.

I am well, working my day shifts; I have explored the sea and I find the fine white sands and the calmness of the water quite exhilarating. During my lunch breaks and after work, I swim at Non Nuoc Beach. Some of my co-workers come along, and we all get on well together.

Believe it or not, like my other colleagues I have grown a full beard. The Yanks have to be cleanshaven, so this is our way of standing out when strolling through town, and not getting a bullet intended for 'the enemy'. Better safe than sorry.

I told you briefly about finding a Vietnamese teacher, and she seems to be helpful and pleasant. Three times a week, we practice phrases and vocabulary in the luxury of my cabin.

As for the local economy, there is very little to write home about. Under the so-called Vietcong, there is a planned economy in the north. When will the communists learn that this does not move a country forward? The Americans want to prevent a domino effect, since a communist victory could lead other countries to follow. This is the reason they are fighting here with such tenacity.

Agriculture is the chief occupation of the Vietnamese, but working in the fields is dangerous. I treat large numbers of landmine victims. Some die and others lose limbs. Those who live go back to the rice paddies. They don't have a choice.

Nevertheless, life in Da Nang is colorful and stimulating. The Vietnamese keep to themselves, but everyone, locals and foreigners, intermixes in the coffee houses and restaurants. By our standards, the traffic is crazy. Four or five people sit on one motorbike, leaving room to spare for a few chickens and fruit on the luggage rack. Besides the local population, I see a lot of GIs in town. They are armed and alert, although their appearance gives the impression they are spending a relaxed evening in the city center. These young guys, clean-shaven and far from home, remind me of being their age, in another war, twenty five years back.

We are living in exciting times. Ho Chi Minh, North Vietnam's president, died three months ago, on September 2.

He succeeded in throwing the French out of his country during the Indochina war, but his fight for an independent communist state prompted the Yanks to act. Their insistence on stamping out communism by any means is their guiding principle, even if the methods they employ are questionable. Every day in the operating theatre, I see the violent results of their mission.

I am in the midst of war, amongst the carnage of death and terror while eventful times occur throughout the rest of the world. This summer, the Americans landed on the moon, the Rolling Stones performed in front of hundreds of thousands in Hyde Park, and the Beatles famously walked over a zebra crossing in north London. Hippy communes have started to appear all over the world, not only in Germany. In California Charles Manson went on a murder spree. A protesting youth culture exists, something previously unimaginable. Today, people talk freely about sex. Public attitudes are changing to a degree I would not have dared to dream. The world is moving at a fast pace, turbulently, and I want to be a part of it. I feel more open-minded and younger than ever before. The blood doesn't run through my veins and organs; it gushes. Herwig, this is the life!!

HEART-TO-HEART CHAT

Remember when you came to Germany on holiday in October 1968 in your big six-cylinder Fiat? You were working as a petroleum engineer in Pau in the Pyrenees, and you wanted to show me all that you had accomplished. By then, the family had moved into our new home in St. Radegund in Austria, though I had stayed alone in Ravensburg for another year. You visited me for two days, and it was during this time that we had one of our rare and memorable conversations. You told me about your work and life, but I dodged all your questions about my past, as I was not ready to talk about it. I have never spoken about the war before, nor about my career as an SS officer, so any bits of information you had then could only have come from your mother. I've never explained the wound on my thigh – when, where, and how I got it.

Following the '68 revolution, many young people like you asked: *'Dad, what did you do during the war?'* Your generation wanted to lift the cloak our society had thrown over the troubled times before and after the war.

Your questions were still unexpected, though, and I was unprepared for them. I had to disappoint you. You accused me of not being sociable, never going to pubs, not being interested in my children, and not sending the girls to grammar school. You blamed me for avoiding all physical contact with my children, for not allowing you to sit on my lap, for never hugging you, and for being emotionally cold. You wanted to know why we moved to the GDR and why we had to move to a different town every few years.

Each time, you and your siblings had to make new friends and felt like outsiders among the locals for a while. What answers did you expect me to give you?

I felt accused of not being interested in culture, never talking about Goethe, Beethoven, or Rembrandt, and not reading novels. You said I had never visited interesting places near our homes, such as St. Radegund when we were at Niederschöckl, or Schwerin Castle near Waren, or Moritz-burg and the Pillnitz Palace when we lived in Dresden. You said you missed having intellectual conversations at home, complained that I spent too much time listening to foreign radio stations, and claimed that I worked too much. I didn't talk, you said. I was a closed book. What did I think of the events unfolding in Europe at the time: the Soviet tanks rolling into Prague?

What did we get out of our conversation that autumn in 1968? You were able to tell me about your experiences; I listened but remained silent about my past.

In the course of this autobiographical letter, I wanted to fill in these gaps. Once you read it, you should be able to answer some questions: 'Who is my father? What kind of a man is he? How should his good and bad sides be seen? What does he think and feel? What angers him, and what frightens him? Does he have a goal, or is he one of life's drifters?'

Josef 'Sepp' Salmutter, MD, 1968

EPILOGUE

Herwig, it is now December 6, 1969, and I am still here in Da Nang. I promised you that I would tell you about my life the way I see it, and now I said it all. It wasn't easy writing this letter, but I am glad I persevered.

I will come to St. Radegund to spend three weeks at the end of January. When we meet there, I will give you my biography, with the accompanying documents, which should help you establish a more comprehensive picture of your father. I had to write it down on paper, as I wouldn't have built up the courage to tell you all of this in person. Would you please hide these documents from Gretl? I'm confident you won't give it to her, but neither should you show it to any of your siblings.

Your brother Wolfgang, five-and-a-half years your junior, is more companionable than you. He often goes out with friends and sings in a band. I never saw much of him. I believe the three girls are close to Gretl, and the two youngest boys, both born in the GDR, can't possibly know me well, being just 12 and 10 years old.

Of all my children, you are the one who knows me best. I was still in my twenties when you and I went out on Sunday mornings to pick mushrooms. I let you ride through the village on my motorbike when you were ten years old. When you were eighteen, the two of us took the train from Dresden to Leoben to find a student flat for you, then on to Klagenfurt to see your grandfather arrange the finance of your studies. Four years later, I came from Ravensburg to Leoben for two days for your graduation. And lastly, there is

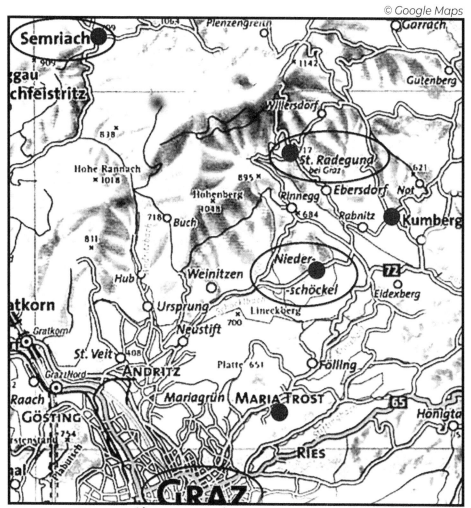

Places of importance in Sepp Salmutter's life:
Semriach - birth,
Niederschöckl - childhood,
Graz - student days, junior doctor,
St. Radegund - family home since 1968

the long conversation we had together last year. I have never spent a single day alone with any of your brothers and sisters.

I never told any of you anything about my past, about my illegitimate birth, or of my SS officer career, as none of you would have understood what it was like to have lived through those times.

You know that I am and have always been passionate about my work. Here in Da Nang, I am appreciated and respected for my competence, which is all I want from my colleagues and the nurses. My job on the ship and newfound freedom have made me happy for the first time since my childhood. As I wrote earlier, I feel renewed with a new zest for life. I am starting to take life in a more relaxed manner. Is this what has enabled me to write you this letter? I don't know the answer, but perhaps.

I am pleased to have brought seven healthy children into the world. I am at peace with myself and have nothing to reproach for. Sometimes I still think of Resi, and of Pasteur's wisdom that she repeated to me. Now I can say, 'Yes. I did what I could.'

Perhaps after you have read my letter, we can talk about my trials and tribulations, my moral dilemmas, and the pleasant and unpleasant turns in my life. In August, during my next holiday, I will be ready to answer any further questions that may arise.

Looking forward to seeing you next month,
Your father,
Da Nang, Vietnam, 6th Dec. 1969

AFTERWORD

Five decades on, I can still remember how I felt as I finished reading my father's autobiography for the first time. I put it down and sat, staring into space, agitated by what I had read. Many thoughts ran through my head. How little I knew of my father!

I needed time to reflect on his letter. On the one hand, I wanted to trust my father's words and believe his life story. On the other hand, I had to accept that my father, on his own admission, had lied to the Americans during the interrogations to present himself in a better light. So had there been other lies, lies he had not confessed to? Could he have lied about his visits to the camps, and what he saw there; worse still, had he participated in atrocities committed by his Division of the Waffen SS?

How was I to judge my father's life? Were the candid descriptions of the sexual affairs in his youth merely a means to persuade me to believe his life story? Had he been so frank with me because I had told him about my exploits in Africa? I was torn.

Should I have spoken straight away to my siblings about the letter? Fifty years would pass before I found myself able to write about my father's eventful life.

Five years after I first read his life story, I flew on a business trip to America, taking the opportunity to travel the short distance from Dulles International Airport to Fort Hunt. On arriving there, I discovered that the army had demolished the extensive complex. This had taken place within a year of my father's interrogation and his nine months of employment in the Translation Service.

The military had maintained the hostile fencing around the former secret detention buildings, landscaped the area with trees and shrubs, and laid out winding paths with parking spaces.

As a secure military zone, 14 miles south of Washington, Fort Hunt now served as a private, |out-of-sight picnic park for senior officers. President Kennedy relaxed there with his family and bathed in the adjacent Potomac River. Later, the army removed all the fencing and handed the site over to the US National Park Service.

Last January, my father would have been 100 years old. It is now over 50 years since he wrote me that letter and that he drowned in the South China Sea. My mother died more than 20 years ago. The passage of time allows for deeply considered reflection.

Indeed, I hesitated long and hard before showing his life story to my siblings as this had been against my father's wishes. I decided to type it word for word into my computer, adding his documents and photos before posting the finished manuscript to each of my six siblings.

Despite having done so, a recurring question plagues my mind, and it will remain unanswered.

Would I have behaved differently in my father's situation?

One thing is sure: I would not have joined the Waffen SS or the Nazi party. In 1939, when my father

This flagpole is dedicated to the Veterans of P.O. Box 1142 who served this country as members of two military intelligence service (MIS) programs during World War II. Their top secret work here at Fort Hunt not only contributed to the Allied Victory, but also led to strategic advances in military intelligence and scientific technology that directly influenced the cold war and space race. The MIS-X program communicated with American military personnel held captive by the enemy Axis forces and attempted to coordinate their escape. The larger MIS-Y program carried out the interrogation of nearly 4,000 enemy prisoners of war and scientists who were processed at this camp.

**Monument at Fort Hunt to the memory
of the US Secret Service**

made his choice, it must have been evident to him, as it had been to everyone else, what the National Socialists stood for:

Racism, based on the Nuremberg Race Laws of 1935

Dictatorship and a one-party state enforcing the removal of Nazi opponents from positions of influence

Coordination ('Gleichschaltung' in Nazi terminology), meaning control over and indoctrination of German society, including media, culture, and education

Is it true that my father lived in a time when 'Madmen led the Blind' – as Shakespeare's King Lear put it – but that he was forced, under such circumstances, to ingratiate himself with the new powers? With more civil courage and moral integrity, he could have found other ways to study at university. His grandmother, his friend Resi, and his German teacher had all advised him not to join the Waffen SS, but he chose not to listen. He had other options.

Today, the question of his support for the National Socialist terror regime remains. To get straight to the point:
Was my father a Nazi?

His voluntary entry into the Waffen SS would indicate that he was. As a member of the Waffen SS, one had to represent, endorse, and propagate National Socialist ideas.

However, my father was only eighteen when he joined the Waffen SS. He did not join the Nazi party, though he would undoubtedly have been encouraged to do so. He was not a fanatical SS man, he was fired from the SS Military Academy in Tölz.

Herwig and Christine Salmutter,
Non Nuoc beach in Da Nang,   Vietnam 2012
where Sepp Salmutter drowned on 30 December 1969

He repeatedly refused to serve in concentration camps. He deserted to the Americans and gave them information about SS officers, higher-ranking Nazis, and concentration camp administrators. after the war, he kept away from all SS veterans' associations.

All the same, I have to live with the fact that my father served in the Waffen SS. How strongly he supported Nazi ideology and to what extent he revised his attitude after the war remains unanswered and unresolved. A trauma I have to live with.

After completing my university studies, I left Austria. Every twenty years or so, I visited Niederschöckl and former childhood friends. I'm glad my father never knew how much it would change! Today it is a satellite town for Graz commuters, with many new houses on tiny plots, the small, traditional country village entirely obliterated.

My great-grandmother's house has been demolished, the cesspit filled in and the old hand-operated water pump that stood in front of her home was removed, the hole filled up and covered in grass. An ugly new house now stands atop the flattened land and a small hut where his grandmother's vegetable garden once stood. The two-lane gravel road running through the village is now asphalted, and there's a regular bus service to Graz.

Weekend hikers still roam through the village and find refreshments at an old converted farmhouse, where the new restaurant owner serves them on rustic wooden tables covered with red-checked tablecloths.

For the ever-increasing number of hikers, the Tivoliweg trail has been sign-posted, leading them up to a hilltop restaurant, where they can enjoy a pleasant view over Niederschöckl.

In the year 2000, at the age of 80, my mother passed away in the St. Radegund family home. All seven of us children took our father's urn, which had been kept inside her bookcase for more than 30 years, to the top of the Schöckl Mountain, where we scattered his ashes to the winds.

Some of it will have blown away to Semriach, the place of his birth; some will have drifted to Niederschöckl, where he spent his childhood, and some will have made their way to Graz, where he went to a Catholic seminary, grammar school, and university.

Father, rest in peace.

Herwig Salmutter,
London 2023

CURRICULUM VITAE
SEPP SALMUTTER

31 Jan 1921   Josef 'Sepp' Salmutter's birth in
Semriach, Austria;
his father remains unknown

9 Feb 1924   death of Sepp Salmutter's mother

1926   move from Semriach to
Niederschöckl, with his
grandmother

1927-1931   school boy in Waldschule,
Niederschöckl, Styria, Austria

1931-1938   Franciscan seminary and Grammar
school, Graz

12 Mar 1938   Anschluss, Austria incorporated into
the German Third Reich

1938-1939   Grammar school boy; acquaintance
with Theresia Egger

Dec 1939   admission to the Waffen SS

Dec 1939-Feb 1940
student 1st trimester at the SS Medical
Academy in Graz

Feb 1940-May 1940
military gunner training in
Berlin-Lichterfelde

Jun 1940-Sep 1940
>front service with the 13. SS Art. Reg.
'Das Reich', paramedic,
SS Unterscharführer, France, Belgium,
Netherlands

Oct 1940-Feb 1941
>student 2nd trimester at the
SS Medical Academy in Graz

Feb 1941-Apr 1941
>SS Military Academy, Tölz, SS Junker

May 1941-Aug 1941
>SS NCO Military Academy, Lauenburg

Sep 1941-Oct 1941
>military training at SS Sanitäts Ersatz
Abteilung, Oranienburg

Nov 1941-Apr 1942
>SS Military Academy, Braunschweig,
SS Junker, appointed to SS officer –
SS Standartenoberjunker

Apr 1942-Jun 1944
>student 3rd to 6th semester at the
SS Medical Academy in Graz;
SS Untersturmführer

27 Feb 1943   marriage to Margarethe Glatz in
Vienna

6 Mar 1943   birth of son Herwig

Jun 1944-Nov 1944
front service, France and Belgium,
2nd SS Medical Company 'Das Reich'

Oct 1944   wounded, grenade shrapnel into
upper thigh, Belgium

Nov 1944   furlough to Graz, after heavy Allied
bombing of his home town

Nov 1944-Jan 1945
Battle of the Bulge, 2nd SS Medical
Company 'Das Reich';
SS Obersturmführer

25 Jan 1945   desertion to US Army in Gouvy,
Belgium

Jan 1945-Apr 1945
POW, handed valuable info to
US Intelligence, Namur, Belgium

9 Apr 1945   transfer to POW camp in USA

Apr 1945-Jan 1946
interrogation by US Intelligence,
Fort Hunt, Virginia, USA,
then working for the US Intelligence
Translation Service

Jan 1946- Feb 1947
POW camp doctor, Columbus,
Wisconsin, USA,
acquaintance with Barbara O'Keefe

Feb 1947-Apr 1947
          POW camp, France

Apr 1947-Nov 1949
          student 7th to 9th semester at the
          Medical University in Graz

Nov 1949   Sepp Salmutter, MD

Nov 1949-Jul 1954
          junior doctor in Graz hospital

Jul 1954-May 1964
          Trauma surgeon, East Germany

Jun 1964-Jul 1969
          Trauma surgeon, West Germany

Aug 1969-Dec 1969
          Trauma surgeon, German Red Cross
          hospital ship 'Helgoland',
          Da Nang, South Vietnam

30 Dec 1969 Sepp Salmutter drowned whilst
          swimming in the South China Sea,
          Da Nang, South Vietnam.

ABOUT THE AUTHOR

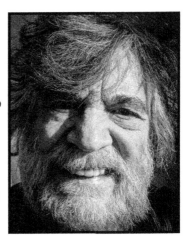

Herwig Hans Salmutter is the eldest son of seven children, coming from two generations of practising medical doctors. He spent his childhood at the end of the Second World War in an impoverished hill village near Graz in Austria where he attended the local Elementary school.

At the age of eleven, in 1954 and at the height of the Cold War his father moved the family to Eastern Germany where the author spent seven years near the Baltic Sea and later in Dresden where he passed his communist Baccalaureate with Russian as his first foreign language. While in Dresden, from the age of 16 to 18, he spent most of his time flying solo gliders having become a member of a paramilitary sports club.

During his time in Eastern Germany, being young and impressionable, propaganda and subtle brainwashing inclined him towards communism. At the age of 18 the author returned to Austria to study Petroleum Engineering at the Mining University of Leoben. By the time he had obtained his Master degree and, following the Russian Red Army march into Prague in 1968 he had thrown off the shackles of any still lingering communist ideology.

Now begins a twenty years odyssey working as a Petroleum Engineer mainly in jungles and deserts around the globe. His first assignment was Cotonou in Dahomey, then Warri in Nigeria, followed by four years in Hassi-Messaoud in the middle of the

262

Algerian Sahara. Tarakan in Indonesia and three years in Ahvaz in Iran under the rule of the Shah of Persia followed. Subsequently Houston, Texas and Calgary in Canada before ending his petroleum career as Vice President ODECO (Gabon) Petroleum Inc. in Port Gentil in Gabon, West Africa.

The author's English wife Christine faithfully shared all overseas assignments creating a peaceful accommodating home space for them wherever they went. She got involved in the established customs, made life-long friends with local women exchanging cooking recipes and garments. She artfully overcame any challenging language struggles.

Working in far-away places could have been times of hardship. Mobil phones did not exist. Phone calls back to Europe had to be organized and could take two days before getting through. The lack of newspapers and English language TV required self reliance and acceptance. Mail took three weeks to arrive. Satellite TV or even video cassettes did not yet exist. Looking back, however, the author believes that these were wonderful years full of exciting experiences and personal happiness.

After twenty years overseas Herwig Salmutter came back to England and a few years later became a naturalised British Citizen. He and his wife started a successful property rental company in London.

The author and his wife have travelled extensively all around the world. They now live in London, UK and in Graz, Austria and share their interest in art history, reading, photography and fine dining in gourmet restaurants.

Herwig Salmutter wrote the book 'Madmen led the Blind', published as a Kindle ebook and as a paperback. He also wrote a close translation in German, 'Tolle führten Blinde', also available on Amazon.

SOURCE REFERENCE

MS Helgoland
-DRK Magazine: Gisela von der Rosen-Panthen 'Doctors and nurses met at the coffins' 20.10.2017
-Dr. med. Alfred Jahn, surgeon on the MS Helgoland, several TV documentaries, conversations with Herwig Salmutter, 2004
-Dr. M.H. Schröer, chief physician on the MS Helgoland, personal letter, dated 23.1.1970

Da Nang
- Herwig Salmutter, Visit and photos from Da Nang, 2012

Namur
- US Intelligence Documents, US National Archives in College Park, Washington

Fort Hunt
-Dr. Felix Römer ,Kameraden - Die Wehrmacht von Innen', Piper, 2012, email correspondence
- US Intelligence Documents, US National Archives in College Park, Washington

Birth
-Diözesanarchiv Graz-Seckau, Pfarre Semriach, Taufbuch 18, S.4, RZ9
-US Intelligence Documents, US National Archives in College Park, Washington

Farm
- Steirisches Landesarchiv, Graz, Grundbuchfolium, Einlage Band 3Q, Seite 97, Niederschöckl, 1925

Ancestors
- Diocesan Archives Graz-Seckau, Parish of Semriach and Maria Trost

Seminary
- Michaela Sohn-Kronthaler, Rudolf K. Höfer, Alois Ruhri' '800 Years Diocese Graz-Seckau', Styria Verlag, 2018

Anschluss
- ©Süddeutsche Zeitung/alamy

Waffen-SS
-Wikipedia 'Organisation of a SS Panzer Division', 2018
-US Intelligence Documents, US National Archives in College Park, Washington

Academy, 1st trimester
- Prof. Mag. Dr. phil. Alois Kernbauer, Research Project, 'SS Medical Academy Graz', University of Graz Archives, Email Correspondence, 2020

Academy, 2nd trimester
- US Intelligence Documents, US National Archives in College Park, Washington

Tölz
- US Intelligence Documents, US National Archives in College Park, Washington

Lauenburg
- US Intelligence Documents, US National Archives in College Park, Washington

Braunschweig
- US Intelligence Documents, US National Archives in College Park, Washington

Academy, 3rd to 6th semester
-Gertraud E. Kaefer-Eysn autobiography 'Medical student Graz 1943'.
-US Intelligence Documents, US National Archives in College Park, Washington

Gretl
- Dr. jur. Gerhard Rainer, unpublished autobiography, 2005

Marriage
- US Intelligence Documents, US National Archives in College Park, Washington

French campaign 1944
-Max Hastings 'Das Reich', The march of the 2nd SS Panzer Division through France, June 1944, Pan Books, 1983
-US Intelligence Documents, US National Archives in College Park, Washington

Special leave
- US Intelligence Documents, US National Archives in College Park, Washington

Battle of the Bulge
-Antony Beevor, Ardennes 1944, Penguin, 2016
-US Intelligence Documents, US National Archives in College Park, Washington

Questionnaire
- US Intelligence Documents, US National Archives in College Park, Washington

Translation Service
- US Intelligence Documents, US National Archives in College Park, Washington

Columbus
-Oconto Country Times Herald, ‚State has surprising history of POW camps', 2011
-Cheyenne Lentz ‚Story of Wisconsin's German POWs is a piece of hidden History', 2015

Austria 1947
-Prof. Helmut Konrad ‚Schicksalsjahr 1945/1955', Kleine Zeitung Essays, Graz, April/May 2020
-Prof. Karin M. Schmidlechner ‚End of the War', Kleine Zeitung Essays, Graz, April/May 2020
-Dr. Heidemarie Uhl ‚Das veruntreute Jahr 1945', Kleine Zeitung Essays, Graz, April/May 2020
-Dr. Wolfgang Maderthaler, Uni Graz, ‚Neuanfang -Österreich nach 1945', Kleine Zeitung Essays, Graz, April/May 2020

-Photo:https://austria-forum.org/af/Wissenssammlungen/
Damals_in_der_Steiermark/Graz_im_Bombenhagel

Denazification at the University of Graz
- Prof. Mag. Dr. phil. Alois Kernbauer, 'From the Imperial
University to the Karl Franzens University

Niederschöckl 1947
-municipality of Weinitzen, email correspondence
University of Graz Archive: Doctoral Certificate, Curriculum,
Photos

German Democratic Republic
- The Federal Commissioner for the Records of the State
Security Service of the former GDR,
letter to Herwig Salmutter, dated 19.08.2020

SEVERAL SELECTED DOCUMENTS

from the full set of 80 pages — US Intelligence Fort Hunt documents — which can be found at

https://hhsalmutter.wixsite.com/sepp1921

SALMUTTER, Sepp
SS Obersturmfuehrer
I./SS Pz Art Regt "Das Reich"
21 Jan '45, GOUVY, Belgium

14 April 1945.

Capt. Brown

    P/W is a young and intelligent Austrian medical officer who deserted to the American forces. He is most cooperative and friendly and, therefore, approachable. He has a magnetic personality with plenty of drive. Believed to be very reliable. P/W worked for FID in NAMUR from the end of January to 5 April 1945.

PERSONAL HISTORY:

    Born 31 January 1921 in SEMRIACH, Steiermark. Mother died in 1924 and father remarried. P/W raised by grandmother, Amalia Salmutter, in NIEDERSCHOECKL/ GRAZ. VS 4 years, Gymnasium 3 years as a pupil of the Franciscan Seminary in GRAZ, Franziskanerplatz 14. The Seminary was closed by law after the Anschluss in 1938. Through friends P/W learned about the SS Aerztliche Akademie (medical academy) which was to be opened shortly in GRAZ, where it would be possible for medical students who were members of the SS to continue their studies with the idea of eventually becoming medical officers in the field. A prerequisite for entrance into the academy was front line service with an SS unit. SS Hauptsturmfuehrer RIENSCH, IV./SS Regt "Der Fuehrer" which was stationed in GRAZ/WETZELSDORF after the Anschluss, and his son, Egon, whom P/W knew at school, urged P/W to take advantage of this offer. No HJ or labor service (RAD).

MILITARY HISTORY:

Dec '39 – Volunteered for Waffen SS.

Feb '40 – Basic training with 2./SS Art Ers. Abt. in BERLIN/LICHTERFELDE.

Feb-Jun '40 – Training as a gunner.

Jun '40 – Front line service (Frontbewachrung) in France with 15./SS Art. Regt, a heavy artillery unit which actually did not see action. FPN 08604.

Jul-Sep '40 – Occupation of the Netherlands near AMERSFOORT.

Oct '40 – Ordered to the SS Aerztliche Akademie in GRAZ. P/W lived at the academy but attended lectures at the University of Graz. Promoted to Oberscharfuehrer (Uffz.)

Feb-Mar '41 – Attended a reserve officers course (Reservefuehrer-bewerberlehrgang) at the SS-Junkerschule TOELZ. Himmler had ordered every company grade medic of the Waffen SS to attend officers' school. Included in this course was an 1/2-hour visit to the concentration camp in DACHAU.

– 1 –

270

Mar '41 — P/W failed the course and received the comment that he was lacking in character to become an SS officer (charakterlich zum SS Fuehrer nicht geeignet).

May-Aug '41 — Because P/W had failed the officers' course, he was ordered to attend the SS NCO school at LAUENBURG/Pommerania for "thorough character and military training", even though he had been an NCO since October 1940.

Sep-Oct '41 — Unterschaffuehrer in SS Sanitaets Ers Amt in BERLIN/ORANIENBURG.

Nov'41-Mar'42 — Attended the officers' training course at the SS Junkersschule in BRAUNSCHWEIG. Included in this course was an 1/2 hour visit to the concentration camp in BUCHENWALD near WEIMAR.

Feb '42 — Promoted to Standartenjunker (Faehnrich).

2 Apr '42 — Deemed worthy to become an SS officer in the medical corps. "Zum SS Fuehrer im Sanitaetsdienste geeignet."

Apr '42 — Promoted to Standartenoberjunker (Oberfaehnrich).

Apr'42-Jun'44 — Continuation of medical studies at the University of Graz as member of the SS Medical Academy.

21 Jun '42 — Commissioned as an SS Untersturmfuehrer (2d Lieutenant).

Feb '43 — Married to non-Aryan Frl. Grete Glatz, also a medical student, and daughter of Obermedizinalrat Dr. Hans Glatz from ST. POELTEN. This marriage caused P/W's SS friends to turn against him and thereafter he always received unpleasant assignments. Request for release from SS not granted.

Feb-Jun '44 — Adjutant of the SS Aerztliche Akademie in GRAZ, in addition to his studies.

30 Jun '44 — Transferred to the invasion front as Asst. Medical Officer of 2. Sanitaets Kp/ SS Pz Div "Das Reich." FPN 34667.

Jun-Sep '44 — Retreat through France and Belgium to the Westwall.

Nov '44 — Transferred to III./SS Pz Art Regt "Das Reich" as medical officer. FPN 15982. This Bn. was just being formed in Westphalia (Sauerland). Promoted to Obersturmfuehrer (1st Lt.)

15-25 Nov '44 — Special furlough to GRAZ because of complete loss of property due to bomb damage. Since the heavy attack on GRAZ in December 1944, P/W has heard nothing from his wife — who resides there.

271

SALMUTTER, Sepp
SS Obersturmfuehrer
I./SS Pz Art Regt "Das Reich"
21 Jan '45, GOUVY, Belgium

P/W is a young and intelligent Austrian medical officer who deserted to the American forces. He is most cooperative and friendly. Believed to be very reliable. P/W worked for FID in NAMUR from the latter part of January to 5 April 1945.

Additional Report on PERSONALITIES:

(Numbers in parentheses indicate approximate ages.)

MAHOULE (36): SS Sturmbannfuehrer; Chief of Security Service (Sicherheits-dienst) in GRAZ. Believed to be a lawyer by profession. Party member. Tall, dark, many sabre wounds in his face. Pampered, vain. Resides in Burgring, GRAZ.

CLEMENS: (33) SS Hauptsturmfuehrer; lawyer and commissioner in the security service. Party member prior to the Auschluss. Tall, blonde, sabre wounds in face; harsh voice. An Austrian by birth; resides in GRAZ. Good friend of SS Sturmbannfuehrer Dr. MITTELBERGER, who from the end of 1943 to beginning of 1944 was commander of the SS Medical Academy in GRAZ.

GREIL, Alfred: (50) Oberstudienrat and Gymnasium teacher. Gymnasium inspector for Styria. Party member prior to the Auschluss. Tall, graying and balding, blue eyes. Native Austrian. Professor of Latin, Greek, and German at the Academic Gymnasium in GRAZ. Illegal head of the Nazi Federation of Teachers in Styria. Active participation in nazification of GRAZ. Resides in GRAZ, Humbaldtstr 29.

GOELLES, Viktor: (50) Oberstudienrat and doctor of philology. Director of the Academic Gymnasium in GRAZ where he resides in Grabenstr. Party member before the Auschluss. Small, dark, wears moustache. Immediately after the annexation he became director of the Academic Gymnasium which was renamed "The First State Gymnasium."

PUCHINGER, Anton: (50) Oberstudienrat and doctor of philology. Director of the "State Gymnasium in GRAZ, Abteilung Graben." Party member prior to the Auschluss. Small, dark, wears a pointed beard. Quiet and reserved type. After the annexation he became the director of the newly-formed State Gymnasium in GRAZ, Abteilung Graben. Resides in GRAZ, Grabenstr 29.

KASPAR, Kurt (?): (45) SS Standartenfuehrer and lawyer. Mayor (Ober-buergermeister) of GRAZ. Party member before the Auschluss. Resides at Grabenstr 90 or 91 in GRAZ. Medium-sized, gray moustache, wears glasses. Enthusiastic member of SS; also belongs to Allgemeine SS. Plays up to high-ranking and influential Nazis. On many occasions has evicted poor Austrian families with many children from their homes in order to provide a dwelling for a high Nazi official. Hated by the people.

UIBERREITHER, Sigfried: (36) SA Brigadefuehrer and lawyer. Gauleiter and Reichsstatthalter of Styria. Party member prior to the Anschluss. Resides in GRAZ. Medium-sized, dark complexion, narrow face, sabre wounds on cheek. SA leader in Styria before the Anschluss. Fanatical follower of Hitler; hated by the people of Styria.

MUELLER-HACCIUS, Otto: (42) SS Oberfuehrer; lawyer and economist. Regierungspraesident of Styria. Party member. Resides in GRAZ. Tall, heavy set, broad face, wears glasses. Prussian and fanatical Nazi. Office in the fortress in GRAZ; handles administrative and secondary school problems.

DADIEU, Armin: (38) SS Standartenfuehrer. Chemistry professor at the University of Graz. Gauhauptmann of Styria. Party member prior to the Anschluss. Resides in GRAZ. Very tall, dark complexion, athletic figure. As a leader in Schuschniggs' VF (Vaterlaendische Front) party he directed the peoples' uprising ("Volkserhebung") in GRAZ in February 1938.

MUELLER, Dr.: (50) SS Oberfuehrer and physician. Division surgeon of SS Geb Jaeg Div "Prinz Eugen." Party member. Resides in the Rainerkogel in GRAZ. Medium-sized, thin. 1940-41 C.O. of the SS Medical Academy in GRAZ. Before the war spent some time in Bolivia. After 1942 became more and more retiring.

KAETHER, Hans: (46) SS Obersturmbannfuehrer and physician. C.O. of the SS Medical Academy in GRAZ until the summer of 1943. Party member; resides in PRAG (?). High government and party connections which he uses to his own advantage. By using his political influence he was successful in placing himself on the staff of the University of Graz for the sole purpose of checking politically on the professors. Took part in many important conferences at the academy. Good connections with the Gestapo. Last seen during the summer of 1943 in GRAZ. Middle-sized, heavy set. Heavy drinker.

MITTELBERGER, Otto Eugen: (40) SS Sturmbannfuehrer and physician. Assistant to the C.O. of the SS Medical Academy in GRAZ. Party member prior to the Anschluss. Resides in Mauerstrasse in GMUNDEN. Fanatical Nazi although a native Austrian. Wanted to become C.O. of the academy. In March 1944 he ordered every member of the academy to contribute 100-RM monthly to the Winter Welfare (Winterhilfswerk). On good terms with the Styrian Gauleiter, Dr. Sigfried Uiberreither, and other officials, especially in the Security Service (Sicherheitsdienst). Medium-sized, dark complexion, several sabre wounds in the face.

SCHLINK, Carl-Edmund: (40) SS Oberfuehrer and physician. C.O. of the SS Medical Academy in GRAZ from April '44 until the present. Resides at Rosenbergguertel 12 in GRAZ. Party member and fanatical Nazi, but as a human being righteous and honorable. Was always having difficulty with his superior, Brigadefuehrer, Dr. Genzken, of the SS Sanitaets Hauptamt. During the occupation of France, in Toulouse as Div. Surgeon for SS Div "Das Reich." An extremely heavy drinker. Tall, dark blonde, excellent military posture, sabre wounds in face. Last seen November 1944 in GRAZ.

von LICHEM, Heinz(?): (38) SS Hauptsturmfuehrer and physician. Head of a course of instruction at the SS Medical Academy. Party member prior to the Anschluss. Resides in PRAG (?). Native of GRAZ but a 150% Nazi who never ceased imitating the Prussians. Hated all Austrians who did not do likewise; very dishonest type. Had himself transferred to the SS Hospital in PRAG in order to gain possession of the house of a liquidated wealthy Czech civilian. Tall, dark complexion, sabre wounds in face, wears glasses. Last seen in GRAZ at the end of 1942.

SKALKA, Egon: (31) SS Hauptsturmfuehrer and physician. Formerly adjutant to SS Obersturmbannfuehrer KAETHER when the latter was C.O. of the SS Medical Academy in GRAZ. Later C.O. of a Medical Co. in SS Pz Div. "Frundsberg." Party member prior to the Anschluss. Resides in KLAGENFURT (?). Native Austrian but has willingly acquired many Prussian mannerisms. Brutal and utterly lacking in scruples. Leads a dissipated and fast life. Extremely ambitious and has a mania for military service ribbons and decorations. Tall, round face, reddish-blonde, short nose, growling voice. Last seen in LeMans in June 1944.

ENGLER, Sigfried: (26) SS Obersturmfuehrer and medical student at the SS Medical Academy in GRAZ. Party member. Resides in SUHLINGEN (HANNOVER). Graduate of a national political educational institution; 150% Nazi; impetuous. Wanted to shoot an American officer and soldiers in the Argentan-Falaise action in August 1944. Tall, long face, barrel-chested, blonde, blue eyes.

SCHMIDT, Ernst: (27) SS Obersturmfuehrer and medical student at the SS Medical Academy in GRAZ. Captured in Normandy by the Americans as a medical officer in the Goetz von Berlichingen Div. Party member; resides in LAUSITZ. Tall, long face with heavy jowls, dark complexion. Fanatical, ambitious and vain Nazi. Once wrote an article on what should be done with Europe ("Wie man's in Europa machen muesste"). One point which was emphasized was that all Poles should be shot.

FORNET, Harald: (26) SS Obersturmfuehrer and medical student at the SS Medical Academy in GRAZ. Medical officer with SS Div "Hitler Jugend" in Normandy. Party member; resides in the Saar territory. Medium-size, dark complexion, prominent eyes, extremely narrow chest. Fanatical Nazi, ambitious and vain. Hates everything Austrian. Thinks of himself as a "superman" and relates proudly how he, a physician, forced some SS men into the attack at Caen at the point of a pistol. Defeated as "educator" of the Hitler Youth in GRAZ.

NIEDER, Peter: (27) SS Obersturmfuehrer and former medical student at the SS Medical Academy in GRAZ. In Normandy 1944 as medical officer with SS Div "Goetz v. Berlichingen." Now P/W in America. Party member; resides in MUENSTER. Tall, blonde, narrow face, typical Nordic type; 100% Nazi. In '44 losing some of fanaticism. Hates Austrians.

Siehe Anlage

Nach diesem Krieg besteht zweifellos eine wesentliche Veraenderung
in der Stimmung zwischen kapitalistischer Bourgeoisie und Arbeiter-
schaft im Vergleich zu den Vorkriegsverhaeltnissen. Nach dem Krieg
kann man von einer schichtmaessig krassen und zahlenmaessig ins Ge-
wicht fallenden Scheidung dieser beiden Vorkriegsextreme ueberhaupt
nicht mehr spreehen. Das Kriegsgeschehen, vor allem die Zerstoerungen
ganzer, grosser Staedte durch Bombardierungen und nicht zuletzt eine
nach dem Krieg zur Auswirkung kommende Inflation vermoegen die Schicht-
unterschiede zwischen der Bewohnerschaft dieser -einstigen- Staedte
fast voellig zu verwischen, und man geht nicht fehl, den offiziell
geschaetzten 95 % des deutschen Volkes, die durch diesen Krieg als
Proletarier-um diesen Ausdruck zu gebrauchen- resultieren, mindestens
75 % des oesterreichischen Volkes als sichin derselben Situation be-
findend gegenueberzustellen(bei dieser Betrachtung nehme ich Oesterreich als etwas mehr zerstoert an als derzeit, aber grosse Verschie-
bungen in den geschaetzten Prozenten werden sich kaum ergeben, da
Oesterreichs geographische und siedlungsmaessige Struktur derart ist,
dass grosse, dicht bevoelkerte Staedte gegen verhaeltnissmaessig duenn
oder ueberhaupt nicht besiedelte Land- oder Gebiergsgegenden stehen;
Wien zum Beispiel stellt mit seiner Bevoelkerungszahl 1 Drittel der
oesterreichischen Gesamtbevoelkerung dar).

Die christlichsoziale Partei ist eine der staerksten Parteien der de-
mokratischen Oesterreich vor dem Anschluss ans Reich gewesen. Ihren
Hauptanhang besass sie in den Landgegenden und den mittleren Staedten,
also Bauern, Handwerker und Buergerstand. Eine Moeglichkeit, ihre vor-
malige Stellung wieder zu erreichen, liegt in der Ermoeglichung ei-
nes dem oesterreichischen Volke einigermassen entsprechenden Lebens-
standards. Ehemalige Funktionaere dieser Partei und die Geistlichkeit
werden diese Partei in ihrem Gerippe nicht unschwer wieder aufbauen
koennen, wenn die vorhin geschilderten Bedingungen zutreffen.

Die Stellung dieser Gruppe zur Rueckkehr der politischen Verbannten
wird sicherlich eine positive sein, denn gerade aus Oesterreich sind
viele Angehoerige der sozialdemokratischen Partei "aus Sicherheits-
gruenden"verschleppt worden.
Was die ausgewiesenen oder verschleppten Juden anbetrifft, so glaube
ich,dass dieselben sicherlich nicht gesetzlich an einer Rueckwanderung
nach Oesterreich gehindert werden duerften.

Das entzieht sich meiner Kenntnis: jedenfalls aber werden diejenigen,
die unter dem Naziregime gelitten haben, nach Aufruf sich sofort melden und auch gerne bereit sein, zu melden, wer sich an ihrem Nachteil
bereichert hat.

Kenne leider keine derartigen Personen naeher, da ich zur Zeit der
Parteiaktivitaeten noch ein Schueler gewesen bin. Sicherlich jedoch
finden sich einige daeon in Konzentrationslagern.

SALMUTTER, Sepp
SS Obersturmfuehrer
I./SS Pz Art Regt "Das Reich"
21 Jan '45, GOUVY, Belgium

3 May 1945.

Capt. Brown

P/W is a young and intelligent Austrian medical officer who deserted to the American forces. He is most cooperative and friendly. He has a magnetic personality. Believed to be very reliable. P/W worked for FID in NAMUR from the latter part of January to 5 April 1945.

MB DAMAGE in GRAZ:

Bomb damage shown on the attached sketch to the east of the MUR river is the result of the attack on 1 November 1944. P/W actually saw this while home on furlough.

Bomb damage shown on the attached sketch to the west of the river is the result of an attack during March 1945. While P/W was in Paris Detention Barracks awaiting shipment to this country, a German lieutenant of mountain infantry who was in GRAZ in March 1945, related the following:

That it was impossible for trains to enter the city. Passengers had to debark in GOESTING because of the complete destruction of rail facilities in GRAZ. That that part of the town west of the river and on both sides of the railroad has been completely destroyed.

Additional explanation of attached sketch:

1. Krefelder Str was formerly Annen Str.
2. Adolf Hitler Platz was formerly Hauptplatz.
3. Troops were quartered in the opera house (#2) during September and October 1944.
4. Along the street running NW from Schiller Platz in the direction of Ruckerlberg there is some further damage to civilian houses.
5. Alte Technik (#5) is the old Technische Hochschule.
6. The Technische Hochschule (#4) is comparatively new.

P/W expressed the opinion that probable military targets for the attack were #3, 4, and 5 on the attached sketch, of which #3 was the only one hit.

276

Report of Interrogation :   6 November 1945
                                                             I/O : Capt. TALLE
P/W   : SALMUTTER, Sepp
Rank : 1st Lt. SS
Unit : 1 Obt.Pz.Arty.Regt.Das Reich
Captd : Gouvy/Belgium, 21 January 1945.

Veracity : Believed reliable.

SECRET

_____ (Grade and arm or service)   10. 21 January 1945 (Date of capture or arrest)

1. Obt. Pz. Arty. Regt., Das Reich (Hostile unit or vessel)   11. Gouvy/Belg. (Place of capture or arrest)

2/ASM-378 (Hostile serial number)   12. Americans (Unit or vessel making capture or arresting agency)

31 January 1921 - Saarlech/Str (Date and country of birth)   13. Medicine Student (Occupation)

_____ (Place of permanent residence)   14. Volk-Gym-Hoch (Education)

Maria Tresch, Grandmother (Name, relationship of nearest relative) 15. English (Knowledge of languages)

Graz/Rieinasse number 32 (Address of above)   16. Good (Physical condition at time of capture or arrest)

One (Number of dependents and relationship)   17. Married (Married or single)

Address of wife and son unknown (Address of above)   18. Gottgläubiger (Religious preference)

ADDITIONAL DATA:

Transferred from	Date depart	Transferred to	Date received	Official signature of receiving officer	Personal effects not transferred

REMARKS: None

SECRET

* If no relative, name person to be notified in case of emergency.
** If personal effects taken from individual are not transferred, note exceptions and place of storage or depot.   24-44392ABC

277

BASIC PERSONNEL RECORD — WORK SHEET
(Alien Enemy or Prisoner of War)   ROOM **B-13**

Internment S.N. **310-2509053**. Name of Internee   **SALMUTTER, Sepp**

Sex **M**. Height **5** Ft. **7** In. Weight **140**. Eyes **Brown**

Skin **Fair**. Hair **Brown**. Age **24 yrs**

Distinguishing marks or characteristics: **Right Thigh, 4 cm scar.**

1. **Obersturmfuehrer**   10. **21 Jan 45**
   (Grade and arm of service)   (Date of capture or arrest)

2. **1 Obt. -Pz. Arty.Rgt.-Das Reich**   11. **Gouvy/Belg.**
   (Hostile unit or vessel)   (Place of capture or arrest)

3. **2/AKA - 375**   12. **(AM)   Coy.   EVG.**
   (Hostile serial number)   (Unit or vessel making capture)

4. **31 Jan 21 - Semriach/Str.**   13. **Medicine Student**
   (Date and country of birth)   (Occupation)

5. _____   14. **(VOL)   SCHUF   (GD) Mech.**
   (Place of permanent residence)   (Education)

6. **Maria Trost, Grandmother**   15. **English**
   *(Name relationship of nearest relative) (Knowledge of language)

7. **Graz/Niedenschoeckel 32**   16. **Good**
   (Address of above)   (Physical condition at time of capture)

8. **One**   17. **Married   S**
   (No. of dependents and relationship)   (Married or single)

9. **Address of Wife and son unknown.**   18. **CAT.   EVG.   (GOD)**
   (Address of above)   (Religious preference)

Previous Camp or Camps prior to Fiery Furnace **By Air**

_____

Namur
Remarks: **In Namur since 21 Jan. TATOO MARKS.**

_____

* If no relative, name person to be notified in case of emergency.

278

SECRET

Report of Interrogation :

P/W : SALMUTTER, Sepp
Rank : 1st Lt. SS
Unit : 1 Obt.Pz.Arty.Regt.Das Reich
Captd : Gouvy/Belgium, 21 January 1945.

5 November 1945
I/O : Capt. HALLE

Veracity : Believed reliable.

Report : Answers to Questionaire submitted by Propaganda Branch 23 October 1945.

Note : Before answering the questionaire, P/W wants to emphasize that he is an Austrian, 25 years of age and that he therefore will discuss the Austrian situation. It can generally be likened to Germany's situation of today, however, except for nominal and insignificant differences.

Ideas about democracy.

1. Do you think Germany can ever become a genuine democracy ? (Explain your opinion).

To 1 : P/W thinks Germany can become a Democracy. In general, the German people have the social and psychological foundation on which a reeducation to democracy can be based. The length of the time in which this goal can be attained depends upon the means used.

2. : Do you think that democracy would be the best form of government for Germany ? (Explain).

To 2 : Yes. P/W thinks that democracy would be the best form of government for Germany. Because of Germany's geographical situation and the international political situation of today, the only alternative to democracy would be totalitarianism, and totalitarianism will also result if the attempt to reestablish a democratic Germany is undertaken by inappropriate means, or if this attempt is not begun soon enough.

Aside from P/W's hope and desire that Germany become a genuine democracy, P/W is afraid that the horrible situation forecast for this winter in Germany may perhaps contribute much to Germany's going Communist. The aftermath of this war will reach its climax this winter. If at this critical and decisive point, where the lives of many German people are at stake, the German Communists (backed by Russia) should be able to undertake measures of relief (with Russian support), they will be very successful in their political intention to build a Soviet Reich especially if they simultaneously denounce the intention of the democratic ("capitalistic") powers not to help Germany, by pointing to the often-expressed statement, let the Germans stew in their own juice, or to the demand, let the United States not play Santa Claus for Europe, especially not for Germany. One should not shut one's eyes to the Bolshevist sense for practical politics and the ability of a totalitarian state to change its course suddenly and unexpectedly on a single order, if such a change is deemed expedient at the time.

3. : What, in your opinion, are the most important characteristics of a democracy (was the Weimar Republic a genuine democracy) ? (What faults do you think it had) Is American democracy a possible model for Germany?).

SECRET

Date **9 Apr 45**
From **1145**
To **1630**
Mon. by **Kiefl**

Sheet **1**
Record

Room Conversation
INTERROGATION
I.O. **Capt Holbrook**
I.O.

Army / Navy
Room **13**
Bldg **B**

P/W 1. **Thümeke** 2. **SALMUTTER** 3.

Quiet

50 Reads Lagerpost – Reading – Trying to locate places
Figure hidden gold in salt mine worth 100 mill
RM – No further comment

a T interrogated by Capt Holbrook to 1425
T Resumes interrogation – factual –
T talks about experiences in captivity in France.
T used to be in "Stahlhelm" – Recalls all the time
he has had to spend (air raid warden etc etc)
in addition to his work – for this was
S is glad he has his Cafe
T talks about evacuating his children

Date 25 April 45
From 2000
To 2200
Tak. by Winter

Cheat 1
record

Room Conversation
INTERROGATION
I.O.
I.O.

Army 1/14
Room
Bldg 4

1. THOMAS   2. SALMUTTER   3.

(S) Teaching English to (T)
"

PW informed of German surrender - talking
about it - seem to be rather glad
(T) Also die Russen werden jetzt Deutschland
vollkommen brschenken, trauten es ihnen
dann leichter fällt das Vertraute Land
für den Kommunismus zu gewinnen
da der Mensch wenn er nichts hat, eher zu
radikalen Mitteln greift.
(S) Jetzt kommt das Kaputte, das Deutsch...
- eine typisch deutsche Angelegenheit.
no R.C.
"

1. Thomas   2. (Schmutter)   3.

0755: Silence

0800 Idle talk. English Language

0830 S.S personalities and idle talk. battle experience, words

0910 ① says SS _____ on 'Nord' fought in Carelia,
under Berner(?) was 25000 strong. 13% losses to a corp
was sent to the West through Norway without losses; as the
front in Norway, Carelia was perfectly static, the violent
fighting in ~~_____~~ France ⚡ was quite a shock to the
officers of the division.

T says his division had only 10000 men.

T Bei Linz war ein KZ. Balduensch(?) in letzter Zeit
aber sie neue KZ aufgebaut für die Familien der ____
die sich ergeben haben.

S Das zeigt die Schwäche des Regimes.

T Die Nazis haben Deutschland vollständig herunter-
gewirtschaftet.

Idle talk fool

T Die SS ~~_____~~ die den Russen in die Hände gefallen sind, brauchen
wir nicht zu beneiden, ich habe gehört alle SS Führer werden
dort ____.

S Wir haben unsere eigene SS Hochschulen die studierten in
Prag Graz. Oberst Blumenritter von Berlin, war der

Salmuther

Ich habe das EK2 selbst verdient — noch
im Krieg kann man sie bestimmt kaufen
o out for Int. (Capt Brown) back 10:15
Hearing room — —
Einige Sachen in meinem Lebenslauf
unklar — wieso Ich in die SS gegangen bin
—das glaubte er mir nicht — er fragte wo
wen sie mir May 41 — er wollte sehen do
h wahrheitsgemäss alles aufgeschrieben
al — Es ist doch so dass man nur die
tzte Einheit im Soldbuch drin hat — be-
onders von den Leuten vom Gen. Stab und
deren Ämtern — —
Das ist doch falsch gerade bei solchen
enten Köpf man mehr Einheiten ein
m keinen Verdacht zu schöpfen —
das war wieder der Hauptmann? —
die führen einen im Umweg zum Verhör
immer — bestimmt mal die I.O's Deutsche
ahrscheinlich Kriegsgefangene — was
achen denn die mit dem Lebenslauf
Ja die laben das auf und im nach
ten Lage schreibt man wieder einen
nd dann vergleichen sie die beiden —
Ich habe für nichts geschrieben —
Das ist noch schwerer weil man dann

283

1. Thümeka   2. Salmutter

after the war, especially since most young
teachers are Nazis. Many others were drafted
[illeg.] P/W. minds being P/W. "man hat's
ganz leicht und bequem"...

Silent

out for int. 1010 - Back 1030

Mit einer vernünftigen Regierung, hätte man
in Januar Schluss machen müssen. —
[from] his experiences in the village, does not
believe an underground Nazi movement will
have popular support except among those
who have nothing to lose". It was rumored
that food supplies, ammo and flak were
being concentrated in South German mountain
region, but P/w says he has no factual
knowledge of such movements ...
"Ich wundere mich bloss, dass sie hier einem
alles so aufs Wort glauben, keine Unterlagen
verlangen. ... Aber es lohnt sich nicht
etwas falsches zu erzählen, sie kommen doch
dahinter. Und dann gehen sie nur strenger vor.
Was punished at Namur for attempting to
send out letters for another P/w.
— Poor Germany! alles ist sinnlos zerstört !
(about his job) His Direktor was Sonder-
ausschuss-Präsident for OKH and Verkehr -
ministerium on Brücke Construction.

284

Printed in Great Britain
by Amazon

25740625R00169